AUG 31 2017

W9-CCR-229

3 1299 00965 2653

THE JOYS OF
JEWISH
PRESERVING

THE JOYS OF
JEWISH
PRESERVING

MODERN RECIPES WITH TRADITIONAL ROOTS,
FOR JAMS, PICKLES, FRUIT BUTTERS, AND MORE—
FOR HOLIDAYS AND EVERY DAY

EMILY PASTER

HARVARD
COMMON
PRESS

Brimming with creative inspiration, how-to projects, and useful information to enrich your everyday life, Quarto Knows is a favourite destination for those pursuing their interests and passions. Visit our site and dig deeper with our books into your area of interest: Quarto Creates, Quarto Cooks, Quarto Homes, Quarto Lives, Quarto Drives, Quarto Explores, Quarto Gifts, or Quarto Kids.

© 2017 Quarto Publishing Group USA Inc.

First Published in 2017 by The Harvard Common Press, an imprint of The Quarto Group, 100 Cummings Center, Suite 265-D, Beverly, MA 01915, USA. T (978) 282-9590 F (978) 283-2742 QuartoKnows.com

All rights reserved. No part of this book may be reproduced in any form without written permission of the copyright owners. All images in this book have been reproduced with the knowledge and prior consent of the artists concerned, and no responsibility is accepted by producer, publisher, or printer for any infringement of copyright or otherwise, arising from the contents of this publication. Every effort has been made to ensure that credits accurately comply with information supplied. We apologize for any inaccuracies that may have occurred and will resolve inaccurate or missing information in a subsequent reprinting of the book.

The Harvard Common Press titles are also available at discount for retail, wholesale, promotional, and bulk purchase. For details, contact the Special Sales Manager by email at specialsales@quarto.com or by mail at The Quarto Group, Attn: Special Sales Manager, 401 Second Avenue North, Suite 310, Minneapolis, MN 55401, USA.

21 20 19 18 17   1 2 3 4 5

ISBN: 978-1-55832-875-4

Digital edition published in 2017.

Library of Congress Cataloging-in-Publication Data available.

Cover and Book Design: Rita Sowins / Sowins Design
Photography: Leigh Olson
Printed in China

FOR ALL THE WOMEN WHO HAVE
COOKED FOR ME—ESPECIALLY
MY GRANDMOTHER HORTENSE PASTER,
MY AUNT ANN BRODY COVE,
AND MY MOTHER GAIL KERN PASTER.

CONTENTS

When I was growing up, for me, being Jewish was far more about food than religion. I was raised in an interfaith family. My father was Jewish, but my mother had been raised Catholic. We did not belong to a church or a temple when I was a child, and I did not have any religious education, save that of the Quaker day school I attended.

We did, however, celebrate Jewish holidays with my father's side of the family. My paternal grandmother, Hortense Paster, was an outstanding cook, and her daughter, my Aunt Ann, went on to have a successful culinary career. These celebrations introduced me to the delights of Ashkenazi Jewish cuisine, but not exactly to religious observance. Our Passover seder featured homemade gefilte fish and outstanding matzo ball soup, but a sketchy retelling of the Passover story. Rosh Hashanah meant a sumptuous dinner with my grandmother's meat-filled kreplach and melt-in-your-mouth brisket, but no actual attendance at religious services. Mind you, my family also had an elaborate Christmas celebration, which reflected my mother's Swedish heritage and had as little to do with religion as our Jewish holiday celebrations did.

Yet, despite my lack of religious observance or education, I always *felt* Jewish. Where I grew up, in Washington, D.C., many of our family friends and my classmates at school were also Jewish. I did not have a bat mitzvah of my own, but I attended one practically every weekend when I was thirteen. I read many books by Jewish authors and about Jewish life. If someone had asked me, I might have even said that I was Jewish, although I would have more likely said I was half-Jewish.

In America, most Jews are Ashkenazi, that is, Eastern European. That was certainly true in my family: my grandparents' ancestors came from Poland. As a result, I had almost no exposure to the world of Sephardic Jewry when I was growing up.

That all changed, when, as a college student majoring in French, I spent my junior year abroad in France. For the first month, a sort of orientation period, I lived with a very traditional, Catholic family in the small city of Tours. I felt uncomfortable in that environment, so when it was time to move to Paris and be placed with our permanent host families, I asked the director of the program not to place me with a religious family. Her response was to place me with perhaps the only Jewish host family in the program, Monsieur and Madame Zémor.

The Zémors were Sephardic Jews who had been born in Algeria and moved to France in the 1950s, when Algeria gained its independence. Living with the Zémors was a wonderful experience. Generous, funny, and blunt, Annie and Charles Zémor showed me what it felt like to be Jewish in a place where Jews were a tiny and somewhat threatened minority. Of course, Jews are a tiny minority in the United States too, but having grown up in an east coast city like Washington, D.C., it never felt that way to me.

Perhaps the most significant part of the experience of living with the Zémors was learning about Sephardic customs and cuisine. Like my grandmother, Annie Zémor was a wonderful Jewish cook, but her repertoire was completely foreign to me. I learned that there was Jewish cuisine beyond gefilte fish, matzo balls, and pastrami; I also witnessed an entirely new, fascinating set of Sephardic traditions and observances, such as a party at the end of Passover to reintroduce flour to the house.

I was so affected by the experience of living with a Jewish family in France, and how different it was from being Jewish in the U.S., that when I returned to college, I wrote one of my law school application essays about it. Little did I know it would be in law school that I would meet and fall in love with a nice Jewish boy, one who would become my husband and with whom I would create a Jewish home and raise two Jewish children.

My husband, Elliot Regenstein, grew up in an observant home regularly attending services at the local Conservative synagogue. He had four Jewish grandparents, including two who had fled Nazi Germany. My in-laws kept a kosher home, and they continue to do so to this day. Indeed, my father-in-law, a food science professor, is a world-renowned expert in the laws of kosher. Marrying someone Jewish and raising Jewish children was a priority for Elliot. While this could have been a barrier to our relationship, given that I was technically not Jewish, I quickly realized I wanted to marry Elliot and I also shared his desire to create a Jewish home.

After years of *feeling* but not really *being* Jewish, when I was in my late twenties, I converted. It was necessary for me to formally convert because my one Jewish parent was my father and Judaism is transmitted through the mother. I also had not received any Jewish education, but I welcomed the opportunity to make up for this deficit. I took classes, studied, and eventually immersed myself in the ritual bath known as the mikveh, the final step of the conversion process. Having completed this process, I was eligible to marry Elliot in a Jewish ceremony officiated by a Conservative rabbi. We were married in 2002.

Since that time, my husband and I have maintained a Jewish home. Today for me, being Jewish is about religion and culture and values. It is also definitely still about food. Food is central to Jewish religious and holiday observances. I enjoy nothing more than hosting friends and family for Rosh Hashanah dinner, a Yom Kippur breakfast, a festive latke party, or a Passover seder. I emulate my grandmother and call my aunt for advice when planning my menu and making traditional family foods. Inspired by my year living with Annie Zémor, I have taught myself about Sephardic cuisine and incorporated some of those dishes into my repertoire as well. I think of myself as first and foremost a Jewish cook.

I began preserving in 2007, inspired by the bounty of my local farmers' market and a desire to eat more locally and seasonally. I started by making jam and pickles, and I soon expanded into preserving relishes, chutneys, fruit butters, and more. I loved the fun, do-it-yourself aspect of home food preservation as well as the flavor of the delicious, wholesome products I made.

Naturally, I soon began combining my home food preservation hobby with my love for traditional Jewish foods. I put up jar after jar of kosher dill pickles and pickled green tomatoes every summer hoping to make enough to last until next year. (Given my family's love for pickles, I never succeeded.) I canned applesauce in September and October that we used to top our Hanukkah latkes in December. And I hoarded jars of apricot jam to fill hamantaschen come Purim. I quickly realized the important role that preserved foods play in traditional Jewish cuisine and began formulating the idea for a Jewish preserving cookbook.

This book is the perfect marriage of my two culinary loves: Jewish cuisine and home food preservation. I researched the history of preserved foods in Jewish cooking and drew inspiration from both Sephardic and Ashkenazi home food preservation traditions. My aim for the recipes was not to simply reproduce historical or traditional recipes. Rather, each recipe is an original creation employing contemporary techniques and ingredients, but still rooted in centuries-old Jewish tradition.

I was inspired by the fruits mentioned in the Bible and the Talmud, life in the shtetls of Poland and Russia, and the abundance of the Sephardic Mediterranean and Middle East. Some of the recipes incorporate ingredients or flavors that are typical of Jewish food; others are inspired by a particular holiday. Still others reflect my family's traditions, as well as the transformative experience I had living with the Zémor family. I was also inspired by the great cooks and eaters in my life, from my Great-Grandma Bessie and her famous cheese blintzes to my Grandpa Al's love of pickled green tomatoes to Annie Zémor's unforgettable matbucha.

Combining my affection for Jewish cuisine with my passion for home food preservation into this collection was a true labor of love for me—one that I hope you will enjoy.

A Jewish Preserving Revival

Home food preservation is experiencing an exciting revival. Concerns about processed foods full of additives, the rise in food allergies and intolerances, and a desire to eat more locally and seasonally have driven home cooks and DIY enthusiasts to make the kinds of foods that their parents once bought without a second thought. People are making their own jams, jellies, pickles, and other preserves using homegrown fruits and vegetables or with local produce from farmers' markets. There are popular blogs devoted to food preservation, and each spring brings a raft of new preserving cookbooks. Cooking schools' summer canning classes fill up with enthusiastic students, and Mason jars sales rise every year. Indeed, sales of the iconic Ball jars have *doubled* since 2001.

At the same time, there is an emerging new Jewish food scene as evidenced by the popularity of delis, Middle Eastern restaurants, and new, Jewish-themed cookbooks. Artisanal Jewish delis are popping up all over the country, including the Mile End Deli and Shelsky's of Brooklyn in New York, Wise Sons Jewish Delicatessen in San Francisco, and Kenny and Zuke's in Portland, Oregon. The few delis and appetizing stores that date back to the emergence of American Jewish cuisine in the early twentieth century are more popular than ever and some, such as the Lower East Side's iconic Russ & Daughters, have expanded their operations. Middle Eastern cuisine is reaching a new and broader audience with the popularity of restaurants and award-winning cookbooks by Israeli-born chefs Yotam Ottolenghi, Michael Solomonov, and Einat Admony. Indeed, new Jewish-themed cookbooks on a wide range of topics appear every year.

I have written this cookbook to update the tradition of Jewish home food preservation for the contemporary cook and DIY kitchen enthusiast. I offer recipes for jams, jellies, pickles, and other preserves that are designed for the way we shop and cook today. The recipes are inspired by the cuisine of the Jewish diaspora. I developed them based on how I cook and preserve: by seeking out fresh fruits and vegetables from the farmers' market; by exploring global ingredients from the Mediterranean, the Middle East, and North Africa; and by observing the holidays and rituals of the Jewish calendar.

You do not need to be Jewish to enjoy and appreciate the recipes in this book. If you are a dedicated canner, these recipes will offer you intriguing flavor combinations, such as Apricot–Poppy Seed Jam (page 41), Apple, Honey, and Rose Water Jam (page 75), and Pink Pickled Hakurei Turnips (page 23), that will send you running to the farmers' market and the Middle Eastern grocer. And the recipes for entrees and baked goods, such as Shakshuka (page 34) and American-Style Cream Cheese Rugelach (page 142), will offer you delicious ways to use your stash of homemade preserves.

If you are a Jewish cook or someone who is interested in Jewish cuisine, but you have not preserved food before, I hope that this book will give you the inspiration you need to learn

an enjoyable and satisfying new skill. I explain the mechanics of water-bath canning in this chapter and give you all the information you need to get started. I am certain that once you do, you will find making your own jams and pickles as easy and as rewarding as I do. (However, if you are still unsure about water-bath canning, you can make any of the canning recipes in this book as refrigerator jams or quick pickles and store them in the refrigerator.)

No matter what path brought you here, I hope that this book will offer you a new and revealing perspective on Jewish cuisine. Together, we can revive the rich tradition of Jewish preserving and make it exciting and relevant for today's home cooks.

WHAT IS JEWISH PRESERVING?

Crunchy kosher dills. Hamantaschen filled with prune lekvar. Date honey. Pomegranate molasses. Foods such as these demonstrate how preserving has played an important role in Jewish cuisine, both Ashkenazi and Sephardic, from Biblical times to today. Preserved foods are a traditional part of many Jewish holidays and celebrations, from date charoset at Passover to applesauce and latkes for Hanukkah.

In the harsh climate of northern Europe and Russia, where Ashkenazi Jews lived for centuries, preserving summer fruits for winter was a matter of necessity, and pickled vegetables livened up an otherwise bland diet. Even today, no Jewish deli in the United States is complete without a dish of pickled cucumbers in various states of sourness on every table.

For Sephardic Jews, preserves and jams made with local fruits, such as quince, figs, and dates, were served from crystal dishes with silver spoons at every joyous occasion. Throughout the Middle East and North Africa, vast spreads of pickled and marinated vegetables were served as part of the meze, appetizers to accompany drinks before meals.

Not only do the Jewish people have a rich culinary tradition, but within that culinary tradition is a long history of preserving fruits and vegetables, a history that we will explore more in this chapter.

The Development of Jewish Cuisine

The development of a distinctive Jewish cuisine is the result of adherence to Jewish dietary laws, known as *kashrut* or kosher, the experience of living in a diaspora, as well as the poverty and isolation that many Jewish communities experienced when confined to ghettos. As they moved from place to place to escape persecution, Jews brought dishes from past homelands to new ones. Those dishes then changed and took on new forms as Jewish cooks made use of local ingredients.

Kosher dietary laws—which forbid pork, shellfish, and the mixing of meat and dairy—require Jewish participation in such tasks as milking, cheese-making, and bread-baking. This pushed Jews into food businesses beginning in ancient times. Because they could not buy wine and food made by Gentiles, Jews produced their own food and wine and they sold it to others. From the Middle Ages on, throughout Europe, it was common to see Jews at local markets selling their handmade foods, including pickles, preserves, and pastries.

The Jewish people are divided into two distinct cultures. One group, the Ashkenazim, settled in northern Europe and Russia. Living in a predominantly Christian culture, the Ashkenazi were forced to converge in ghettos and distinct villages, known as *shtetls*, leading to their isolation from their neighbors. The second group, the Sephardim first settled in Spain and Portugal, where they thrived for many centuries. But after the Spanish Inquisition, they were dispersed to Italy, North Africa, the Middle East, and Central Asia. As a result, the Sephardim were mostly under Islamic rule. The Sephardim lived in cities and mingled more freely with their non-Jewish neighbors.

These two cultures developed two distinct cuisines, each with their own interpretation of Jewish dietary laws, that was naturally influenced by the ingredients available to them and the cuisines of their neighbors. Yet, there are uniquely Jewish foods based on local ingredients that still share strong similarities to Jewish dishes from other parts of the diaspora because of similar dietary prohibitions and holiday traditions.

More recently, a third category of Jews, the Mizrahim, has been identified for those who trace their ancestry to the Middle East, as opposed to the Iberian peninsula. Sephardic Jews fleeing Spain sometimes ended up in the same areas as Mizrahi Jews. From a culinary perspective, the Mizrahi and Sephardim share many traditions and had access to similar ingredients.

Many scholars believe that the kosher laws contributed to the survival and distinctiveness of the Jewish people because they created commonality between all Jewish communities, no matter now far apart they were geographically or how different their surroundings were. Indeed, while Jews throughout the diaspora were influenced by the ingredients and cooking techniques of their neighbors, the dietary laws kept their kitchens distinct. The kosher laws also meant that we know a lot about the history of Jewish culinary customs: debates over the interpretation of the laws meant a lot of discussion of food in Rabbinic literature.

The Laws of Kosher

The strictures of the kosher laws, as well as the necessary separation and self-reliance that those laws required, is one of the defining characteristics of Jewish cuisine. For those of you who are not familiar with the kosher laws, I offer a brief overview. I am by no means an expert on kosher, nor do I keep kosher myself. Although this is not intended as a kosher cookbook, as it happens, most of the recipes in this book are easy to make for someone who observes the kosher laws because they are all vegetarian and only a few even use eggs or dairy products.

Kosher simply means "fit" or "proper for consumption." The kosher dietary laws are not health or hygiene requirements. Rather, they provide a framework for the culinary practices of people of the Jewish faith. A Jew who observes the laws of kosher cannot eat food from a kitchen, be it in a restaurant or someone home's, that does not adhere to these rules. The dietary laws are a sign of Jews' special relationship with God. Obedience to them is a show of devotion and is believed to turn an ordinary meal into a sacrament.

Most kosher laws affect products from the animal kingdom. These laws govern which animals can be eaten, how animals must be killed and prepared for eating, and the separation of milk and meat. For our purposes, the most significant of these rules concerns the separation of milk and meat. The Bible instructs: "Thou shalt not seethe the kid in the milk of its mother." That phrase has been interpreted to mean that, as a practical matter, all cooking facilities and all food preparation equipment, including serving and eating utensils, must be separated by whether they are used for milk or for meat. Under the kosher laws, Jews are required to wait several hours after consuming meat before consuming milk again; there is no required waiting period after consuming milk to consume meat, although some Jews observe one.

Neutral foods that are neither milk nor meat are called *pareve*. All plant foods are pareve, along with eggs, fish, and honey. Pareve foods can be prepared and eaten with dishes containing either milk or meat. There are, however, several rules that affect the consumption of plants and other pareve foods. For example, because of the prohibition on eating insects, if the edi-

ble part of a fruit, vegetable, or grain is subject to insect infestation, the product must be carefully checked to be sure there are no "visible" insects.

In addition, someone who observes the Sabbath, that is to say, an observant Jew, must participate in the milking of animals, making dairy products, such as cheese, and baking. Also, breads baked with a significant quantity of five specified grains—wheat, rye, oats, barley, and spelt—must also have a small portion of the dough removed as a symbolic act of sacrifice.

There are additional restrictions for the observance of Passover. During Passover, Jews are prohibited from eating the same five major grains in any form other than unleavened bread known as matzo.

These dietary laws are at least in part responsible for the rich and distinctive tradition of Jewish preserving. Because of the difficulty of finding foods prepared by others that fulfilled kosher requirements, Jews made most, if not all, of their own food. Many continued to do so even after commercially prepared versions became readily available to ensure that they were not running afoul of these principles. In addition, the kosher prohibition on mixing meat and dairy foods, not only in the same dish but in the same meal, made fruits, and to a lesser extent nuts, the typical way to end a meal, even a holiday or festival meal. Thus, it was important to preserve fruits by drying them or by turning them into jams, pastes, and fruit butters for the times when fruit was not in season.

Food Preservation in Jewish Cuisine

In a time before refrigeration and convenient cargo transport, when foods could not readily be shipped from one part of the world to another, home food preservation was a necessity for all people. Summer fruits were preserved for winter by dehydration or in jams and jellies; summer and fall vegetables were pickled and fermented; and meat and fish were smoked, dried, and pickled.

The tradition of Jewish food preservation begins in the Bible. Among the foods mentioned in the Jewish Bible are dates, pomegranates, grapes, and figs—all of which would have been preserved. Indeed, it is believed that the honey referred to in the phrase "the land of milk and honey" is actually date syrup because there is no evidence that Biblical people kept bees to make honey. The Bible also talks about how wine for religious ceremonies could be made from fermented dates, figs, and pomegranates, as well as from grapes. And vinegar made from wine was used for pickling.

But what we think of as Jewish cuisine today bears little resemblance to Biblical cooking. It was in the diaspora that Jewish cooking, in its many forms, came to be. And indeed, other than the adherence to the kosher laws, the central feature of Jewish cuisine is adaptation. Both Ashkenazi and Sephardic Jews developed their own food preservation traditions based on the agricultural products of their region. The harsh climate of northern and eastern Europe, where the Ashkenazi Jews lived, made them reliant on preserved foods to survive. The abundant fruits of summer, such as apples, pears, plums, cherries, gooseberries, currants, and raspberries, were turned into jam and syrups for winter. The vegetables available to the Ashkenazim were mostly root vegetables, but what could be preserved, such as beets, cabbages, and cucumbers, were pickled not only as a method of preservation, but also because tangy pickles were a welcome contrast to the blandness of the rest of their winter diet.

The Sephardim typically lived in areas where the climate was milder, the growing season longer, and the agricultural bounty richer. Nevertheless, food preservation was still very much part of the culinary tradition. Sephardic women would gather at the end of the growing season to make large quantities of preserves to last their families through the year. There was a tradition in the Sephardic world of offering fruit preserves to guests with elaborate ceremony using crystal bowls on silver trays, silver spoons, and glasses of ice water. These same preserves were also brought out on happy occasions, including the new year, as a way to surround the celebrants with sweetness. Sephardic preserves were made with rose petals, quince, orange, apricot, date, and fig, and even vegetables, such as pumpkin, squash, and carrot. Pickles and marinated vegetables also had an important place in the Sephardic world: they were served as meze with drinks and then again as side dishes during the meal.

Of course, non-Jewish families in these same parts of the world, eastern Europe, Russia, the Mediterranean, and Middle East, also had a tradition of preserving food. What makes Jewish food preservation distinctive? First, because of the kosher dietary laws, Jews were more likely than non-Jews to make their own foods, including preserves, even when commercial varieties became available. Indeed, kosher laws prohibited pickled vegetables containing wine or vinegar obtained from or prepared by non-Jews. Thus, the Jewish preserving tradition is particularly robust. In some ways, Jews were the original DIY kitchen enthusiasts.

In addition, Jews have always relied heavily on fruit-based desserts, such as jam, fruit in syrup, or compote made from dried fruits. Due to the kosher laws, after a meat meal, no dairy-based desserts could be served, including pastries baked with butter or served with cream. Until modern inventions, such as Crisco and dairy-free margarine, the prohibition on mixing meat and dairy significantly limited the kind of sweets that Jews could serve after a meat meal and made fruit, whether fresh or preserved, the typical after-meal treat.

Today, when we think of traditional Jewish foods, many of them include preserved fruits and vegetables. Think about a kosher dill pickle or the sauerkraut on a Reuben sandwich, or apricot jam in rugelach, or the applesauce on top of a Hanukkah latke. These iconic Jewish foods demonstrate how important preserves are to Jewish cuisine. But they are just the beginning. As you will see when you explore the recipes in this book, the world of Jewish home food preservation is rich, varied, and inspiring.

Preserving throughout the Year:
The Jewish Holidays

For Jewish families, cooking has always revolved around the Sabbath and religious festivals. There are special foods for every kind of celebration from the complete change in diet at Passover to the far less dramatic traditions of ringing in the new year with sweet foods or eating poppy seeds at Purim.

Preserves play an important role in many of these holidays. In earlier times, much of the preserving activity in Jewish homes was part of the preparation for various festivals: Rosh Hashanah was not complete without home-pickled cucumbers for the Ashkenazim or saffron-colored pumpkin jam for the Sephardim. Passover meant preparing pots of *eingemacht*, a conserve of fruits and nuts suspended in a thick syrup, or *halek*, a date jam that Middle Eastern Jews used as charoset. It is these special holiday preserves, which often have a connection to a Biblical story or an ancient custom, that make Jewish home food preservation particularly distinctive.

Throughout the book, I will note when a particular preserve is part of a traditional holiday celebration or was inspired by a holiday food. For those of you who are not familiar with the Jewish calendar, here is a short description of the major holidays and festivals that are associated with food and how we celebrate them.

ROSH HASHANAH

Rosh Hashanah, which means the head of the year, is the Jewish new year. Like many new year celebrations, it is joyous and festive. However, Rosh Hashanah also ushers in a solemn ten-day period of introspection, known as the Days of Repentance. It culminates with Yom Kippur, the Day of Atonement, and is marked by a daylong fast.

There are many traditional Rosh Hashanah foods, often with symbolic meanings. The most common Rosh Hashanah tradition, and one that is consistent across the entire Jewish diaspora, is to eat sweet foods to symbolize the hope for a sweet new year. Ashkenazi Jews, for example, often begin the Rosh Hashanah meal by dipping slices of apple in honey. Quince is the traditional Rosh Hashanah fruit for Sephardic Jews.

Other foods are traditional because eating them is considered to be a good omen for the new year, bringing luck and prosperity. These traditions are often based on a food's color or appearance or, more obscurely, they are a play on the Hebrew or Yiddish name for the food.

SUCCOT

Like Passover and Shavuot, Succot is an agricultural festival and is linked to the exodus from Egypt. Succot comes close on the heels of Yom Kippur and marks the traditional time of the fall grain harvest. Some people think of it as a Jewish Thanksgiving. The observance of Succot incorporates some charming customs. Families—or, more commonly these days in Reform Judaism, congregations—construct an outdoor temporary shelter, known as a Sukkah, with an open, thatched roof, similar to the temporary shelters used during the ancient grain harvest. This is done to commemorate the forty years that our ancestors spent wandering in the desert without permanent homes. Decorating and dining in the Sukkah is part of the holiday's observance. The second important ritual of Succot is reciting a blessing while waving two special items. The first item is a cluster of branches, taken from a date palm tree, a willow, and a myrtle, which is known as a lulav. The second is a large citrus fruit, known as an etrog.

HANUKKAH

Hanukkah, the Festival of Lights, commemorates the victory of a small group of Jews, the Maccabees, over the army of the Syrian-Greek King Antiochus in the second century BCE. After the Jews drove the Greeks out of Judea, they attempted to restore their temple, which had been destroyed in the war, but discovered that there was only enough oil to light the lamp that held the eternal flame for one day. The story is that a miracle occurred and the oil lasted for eight days, which was how long it took to make new oil. That is why Hanukkah lasts for eight days.

It is traditional therefore to celebrate the holiday by eating food cooked in oil. In Israel, they eat jelly doughnuts called *sufganiyot*, and Sephardic Jews make dough fritters called *bañuelos* that are similar to beignets. The most well-known Hanukkah food for Eastern European Jews are potato pancakes called *latkes* that are traditionally served with applesauce.

TU B'SHEVAT

Tu B'Shevat is a minor Jewish festival at the beginning of the Biblical agricultural cycle known as the New Year for trees. In ancient times, worshippers brought fruit offerings to the temple on this day. During the Renaissance, Jewish mystics created a new ritual to mark the festival with a meal that was modeled on a Passover seder. At this meal, participants ate fruits and grains associated with the land of Israel, including wheat, barley, grapes, figs, and pomegranates, and they drank ceremonial glasses of wine. Sephardic Jews continued to celebrate Tu B'Shevat for centuries with feasts and visiting, while the Ashkenazis Jews, for whom Tu B'Shebat fell in the depths of winter, barely marked it.

Today, most American Jews think of Tu B'Shevat, if they think of it at all, as Jewish Arbor Day. Many people mark the day by planting a tree or donating money for a tree to be planted in Israel. It is a day for affirming the Jewish people's commitment to environmental stewardship.

PURIM

Purim, the Jewish carnival festival, commemorates the salvation of the Jewish people in ancient Persia from an evil government minister, Haman, who planned to destroy them. The story begins when King Ahasuerus sets aside his queen Vashti and marries the beautiful Esther who, unbeknownst to the king, is Jewish. Haman, the king's most important minister, hates the Jews because they refuse to bow to him, and he plots to kill them. Esther reveals to the king that she herself is Jewish and exposes Haman's plot. The king orders that Haman be hanged on the very gallows he built for the Jews, and the Jewish people are saved.

Jews celebrate Purim by reading the Book of Esther, which is in the form of a megillah, or scroll. This is a noisy business because everyone boos, hisses, or shakes groggers whenever the name of the villainous Haman is mentioned. Congregations encourage their members to come in costume to hear the reading of the Megillah, leading some to call Purim the Jewish Mardi Gras. (It is often around the same time of year as that other carnival holiday.) Eating, drinking—to excess even—and generally making merry are all part of the Purim festival. Another Purim tradition is the giving of edible gifts called *michlach manot*.

PASSOVER

Passover, which commemorates the Jews' exodus from Egypt in the time of the Pharaohs, is one of the most important periods in the Jewish year. Indeed, Passover is the most widely celebrated holiday among the Jewish people. The center of the festivities is a ritual meal, usually observed on the first two nights of the eight-day long holiday, called a *seder*, a word that means "order" in Hebrew. The seder participants follow a prescribed order of rituals and ceremonies, many of which incorporate symbolic foods, that is set forth in a special book called the *Haggadah*.

During the eight days of Passover, observant Jews are forbidden to eat any foods containing *chametz*, which are foods made with wheat, rye, oats, or barley, except for matzo, a flat, cracker-like bread, as well as any leavened foods. These restrictions have given rise to an entire culinary sub-tradition of Passover foods: some incorporate matzo, such as matzo balls, matzo brei, and matzo meal pancakes, and others simply rely on alternate ingredients or forms of leavening, such as desserts made with coconut, beaten egg whites, or nut flours.

SHAVUOT

Coming fifty days after Passover, Shavuot, which means "weeks" in Hebrew, commemorates the day God gave the Torah, including the Ten Commandments, to the nation of Israel at Mount Sinai, and marks the Biblical wheat harvest. There are no specific requirements for celebrating Shavuot—unlike the many required observances for Passover, for example—but there are many *minhagim*, or customs, associated with the joyous festival.

One of the primary customs, particularly among the Ashkenazi, is the consumption of dairy foods. The origin of this tradition is not entirely clear. It may simply be that Shavuot occurs during the spring, which is the season when cows calve and give milk. The religious explanation is that once the Jews received the Torah, which laid out the kosher dietary laws, they could not eat any of their previously prepared meat dishes nor could they prepare any meat until they had cleansed their utensils. Thus, they were forced to eat dairy. Traditional Ashkenazi dairy dishes for Shavuot include cheesecake, cheese-filled crepes (known as blintzes), noodle kugel, and triangular cheese-filled dumplings called *kreplach*.

To celebrate the harvest aspect of the holiday, many Jews decorate their synagogues and homes with greenery and flowers during Shavuot. In the Middle East, the synagogues are decorated with rose petals, and Shavuot is known as the Festival of the Roses. Thus, for Jews from this part of the world, many Shavuot foods are flavored with rose water.

Don't Be a Shiterein Cook: ***Safe Water-Bath Canning Procedures***

In Yiddish, someone who cooks from experience and touch without referring to recipes or measurements is called a *shiterein* cook. That's a wonderful quality when you're making chicken soup or brisket, but not so much when canning food to be shelf-stable. When preserving fruits and vegetables, follow tested recipes to ensure that your jams and pickles are safe to can using the boiling water-bath method. Moreover, when making jam in particular, if you don't maintain the correct ratios of fruit to sugar, you will have difficulty achieving a spreadable texture.

If you are new to preserving food this way, this explanation will give you enough information to get started with confidence. Water-bath canning may seem intimidating at first, but it is easy to learn. After you do it a few times, it will become second nature. If you are an experienced canner, please review these instructions. It is always a good idea to remind yourself of the proper techniques before undertaking a new canning project.

First, water-bath canning is a safe method of home food preservation for foods below pH 4.6, or high-acid foods. You can water-bath can foods that are naturally high in acidity, such as many fruits, or by introducing acid into the product in the form of lemon juice or vinegar. That is why, for example, to safely can a low-acid food, such as carrots or cucumbers, you need to do so using a vinegar brine or, in other words, to pickle it. All new canners fear botulism, but it cannot live in a high-acid environment. Thus, if you adhere to tested recipes, you need not be concerned about botulism.

In water-bath canning, filled jars are placed in a bath of boiling water for a specified amount of time, depending on the recipe. The heat from the water penetrates the jars to kill any bacteria, and oxygen escapes from the jars to create a vacuum seal that will make those jars shelf-stable. To achieve this result, you must use the correct equipment: a large pot outfitted with a rack that will allow the boiling water to circulate all the way around the jars, including underneath, and glass canning jars with lids that seal. You should only use glass canning jars that are either new or in excellent used condition, without any cracks or nicks, and lids that are intended for home canning use.

Glass jars do not need to be sterilized before filling so long as the final product will be processed in the boiling water bath for ten minutes or more. (For refrigerator pickles and other recipes that are not canned, of which there are several in this book, it is important to sterilize the jars before use by filling them with boiling water, emptying them, and allowing them to air-dry.)

To begin a preserving project, fill your canning pot with water and place the number of empty jars that you will need in the pot. While you do not need to sterilize the jars, you do need the jars to be clean and warm before filling them. If you ladle hot jam or pickling brine into a cold or even room temperature jar, the jar could crack. Bring the water to a boil while you pre-pare the food. If the water boils before you are finished, simply turn the heat down and keep the water at a simmer until you are ready.

When the food to be preserved is ready, remove a jar from the water, empty it, and fill it with the preserve. If making a jam or spread, simply ladle the spread into the jar. If making a pickle, first pack the vegetables into the jar, as tightly as possible without damaging them, and then ladle the brine over the vegetables. I recommend using a funnel when filling jars to mini-mize spilling and waste.

It is critical not to fill the jar to the top. This extra room at the top of the jar is known as the headspace. Every recipe in this book specifies how much headspace to leave, from ¼ inch (6 mm) in jam recipes to as much as ¾ inch (2 cm) or a full inch (2.5 cm) in other types of preserves.

Failing to leave enough headspace could cause the jar to overflow, and that might prevent the lids from sealing. Do not leave less headspace than called for, but do not leave more either. A jar that is only partially filled cannot be safely processed because all of the oxygen might not escape during the processing time. Store any partially filled jars in the refrigerator or transfer the product to a smaller jar for processing.

After the jar is filled, run a thin plastic utensil around the inside of the jar to release any air bubbles. This is known as bubbling the jars. Lastly, clean off the rim of the jar with a damp cloth because any residue that is left on the rim could prevent the lid from sealing. Then place the lid on the jar and tighten it just until you feel resistance. This is known as fingertip-tight. Do not close the lid too tightly because that could prevent any air inside from escaping.

The jar then goes back into the boiling water. Make sure that the water covers the top of the jar by several inches (18 mm). The jar should remain in the boiling water bath for the time specified in the recipe, typically ten minutes for jam and fruit spreads and fifteen minutes for pickles. This is known as the processing time. If the water is not boiling when you put the jars in it, do not begin to count the processing time until the water has returned to a boil.

After the jars have been processed in the boiling water bath for the requisite amount of time, turn off the heat and remove the top. Allow the jars to remain in the water for a few minutes to cool slightly. After a few minutes, remove the jars to a towel, which will insulate them from the cold countertop and absorb any excess water. The jars should cool undisturbed for several hours. You may hear a ping as the jars seal, but do not be dismayed if you do not: the jars may still seal without the noise. Once the jars are cool, ensure that the button in the middle is pressed down or concave. If so, then the seal is good.

What if your jars did not seal? A failure to seal could be the result of residue left on the jar rim, overfilling the jars, or simply a bad lid. If a jar's lid does not seal, that simply means that the food inside is not shelf-stable. The food is still good, however, so definitely do not discard it. Store the jar in the refrigerator instead.

Sealed jars can be stored without refrigeration for up to one year. Light and heat will cause the products in the jars to lose flavor, although they are still safe to eat as long as the seal is good. So I recommend storing jars in a cool, dark place. Once open, jars should be stored in the refrigerator.

For best results, adhere to the ingredient amounts in this book's recipes. If a particular recipe makes a larger quantity of jars than you wish, halve the recipe, maintaining the same ratios. However, do not double the recipes, especially for jams and jellies. If the quantities are too large, the spread may never gel.

CHAPTER 1

JAMS, SYRUPS, BUTTERS, AND OTHER FRUIT PRESERVES

This chapter primarily contains recipes for sweet fruit spreads, syrups, and preserves inspired by the fruits, the flavors, and the celebrations of the Jewish diaspora. There are also a few savory fruit-based recipes and a few sweet vegetable-based recipes.

When preserving, you will always have the best results with in-season, local fruits. Some of the recipes call for fruits that can be hard to source, such as currants or quince. Your best chance of finding these is at your local farmers' market. I offer suggestions on where to source any fruit that is not readily available at your local grocery store.

A few of the recipes rely on dried fruits—which have always been a popular ingredient in Jewish cuisine—and therefore are appropriate for year-round canning. Other recipes incorporate citrus fruits, which played a significant role in the history of the Jewish people—or should I say, the Jewish people have played a significant role in the history of citrus. The best citrus fruits are available during the winter. So you should find a canning project in this chapter for any month of the year.

When making jam, the goal is to achieve a spreadable, gelled consistency. Sometimes canners add pectin to their jams to facilitate gelling. Pectin is a naturally occurring substance that gives fruit its structure; when cooked with sugar and acid, it causes fruit spreads to gel. Some fruits are naturally high in pectin and others are not. As a nod to traditional methods of making jam, none of the recipes in this book call for additional pectin. Thus, you need to cook the jam recipes to the gelling point of 220°F (104°C). A candy thermometer is useful for this process.

There are also many old-fashioned ways to test whether your preserve has gelled. One method that I like is the freezer test: Place a saucer in the freezer when you begin cooking your preserve. When you think the preserve is done, place a small dab on the chilled saucer and return it to the freezer for one minute. Then, remove the saucer and push the preserve with your finger. If it wrinkles and appears to be set, it is ready.

Due to the lack of added pectin, some of the jams in this book have a softer set than store-bought jam. That is commonplace for many typical Jewish preserves, particularly Sephardic and Russian jams which were traditionally eaten with a spoon as opposed to spread on bread. These soft-set jams are both delicious and versatile.

POLISH STRAWBERRY RHUBARB JAM

My father's family hails from Poland: Krakow to be exact. Both strawberries and rhubarb grow abundantly in Poland, coming into season in June. Rhubarb is a favorite among Eastern Europeans, and it finds its way into everything from beverages and soups to compotes and desserts. It is tart and so is usually combined with other fruit or the quintessential Eastern European sweetener, honey.

This jam has a soft set because both strawberries and rhubarb are low in acid and pectin. Lemon juice adds some much-needed acidity. Because of its runny consistency, this jam is lovely as a topping for cheese blintzes. Happily, the traditional holiday for serving blintzes, Shavuot, often falls during late spring—peak strawberry and rhubarb season.

4 cups (488 g) sliced rhubarb

4 cups (680 g) lightly crushed
  strawberries

2 lemons

5 cups (1 kg) sugar

»» MAKES SIX 8-OUNCE (235 ML) JARS «««

Prepare a boiling water bath and heat six 8-ounce (235 ml) jars. Place a saucer in the freezer to chill. Zest and juice the lemons, reserving the rind and seeds.

Combine the rhubarb, strawberries, lemon zest, and lemon juice in a large, deep saucepan. Tie the rinds and seeds in cheesecloth and add to the pot; this will add pectin to the jam and help it set.

Bring to a boil over high heat. Reduce the heat to medium-high and boil until the rhubarb breaks down, about 5 minutes, stirring constantly. Add the sugar all at once and return to a boil, stirring constantly. Boil until the jam begins to come off a spoon in a thick stream rather than droplets, between 15 and 30 minutes.

Remove the saucer from the freezer. Place a dollop of jam on it and return it to the freezer for 1 minute. Remove the saucer and push the jam with your finger. If it wrinkles, then it is set. (It will be a soft-set jam.) If not, continue to cook the jam and try the test again after a few minutes.

Remove the jam from the heat and skim off any foam. Ladle the jam into the clean, warm jars, leaving ¼ inch (6 mm) of headspace. Bubble the jars and wipe the rims with a damp cloth. Place the lids on the jars and screw on the rings just until you feel resistance. Process the jars in a boiling water bath for 10 minutes. Allow to cool in the water for 5 minutes before removing. Store in a cool, dark place for up to 1 year.

RED CURRANT AND KIDDUSH WINE JELLY

Tart, tiny red currants may be foreign to most Americans, but Europeans cook with them frequently. Currants are a hardy crop and easy to grow, making them ideal for the harsh climate of eastern and northern Europe. They grow abundantly in Poland and Russia, where they have been cultivated since the eleventh century, and the fruits appear in all kinds of preserves and desserts from that region.

Red currant jelly is an old-fashioned confection that is used to glaze fruit tarts or strawberries. It also works well in savory dishes. Indeed, red currant jelly is used to make Cumberland sauce, a classic British accompaniment to game and lamb.

Here, I combine juice from red currants with a fruity red wine to create a rich, plummy, but still tart, jelly. I like to use sweet kiddush wine, such as Manischevitz—usually the bottle that has been sitting in the refrigerator since Passover. But any sweet, fruity red wine will do. This jelly goes very well with cheese. You can also use it as part of the gravy in your favorite brisket recipe.

2½ pounds (1.2 kg) red currants, stems removed (Stems can impart a bitter flavor.)
2 cups (475 ml) fruity red wine
Rind of 1 orange
1 cinnamon stick
Sugar (amount will vary)

Note: Fresh currants are not to be confused with the small dried fruit of the same name, which are actually dried grapes. Currants grow on shrubs.

»» MAKES TWO 8-OUNCE (235 ML) JARS ««

Combine the currants, wine, orange rind, and cinnamon stick in a large saucepan. Bring to a boil over medium heat and boil gently for 30 minutes, mashing the currants a bit to help release their juices.

Set a fine-mesh sieve lined with cheesecloth or a jelly bag over a deep bowl. Ladle the currant mixture into the sieve or jelly bag and allow to drain undisturbed for at least 6 hours or overnight. Do not press on the fruit to extract more juice because that can cause cloudiness. The following day, prepare a boiling water bath and heat three 8-ounce (235 ml) jars. Place a saucer in the freezer to chill.

Measure the liquid in the bowl. In a large saucepan, combine the juice with an equal amount of sugar. Bring the mixture to a boil over medium heat. Boil for 5 minutes. This jelly gels quickly because of the high pectin content of currants.

Remove the saucer from the freezer and place a dollop of jelly on it. Return it to the freezer for 1 minute. Remove the saucer and push the dollop with your finger. If it wrinkles, then the jelly is set. If not, continue to cook the jelly and try the test again after a few minutes.

Remove the jelly from the heat and skim off any foam. Ladle the jelly into the clean, warm jars, leaving ¼ inch (6 mm) of headspace at the top. Bubble the jars and wipe the rims with a damp cloth. Place the lids on the jars and screw on the rings just until you feel resistance. Process the jars in a boiling water bath for 10 minutes. Allow to cool in the water for 5 minutes before removing. Store in a cool, dark place for up to 1 year.

RASPBERRY RED CURRANT JAM

Red currants are an excellent source of vitamin C, a fact which my Polish ancestors could not have known. But they certainly knew that these tiny berries had medicinal properties. In the shtetl, currant and berry syrups were often administered as tonics to the sick and weak. Interestingly, one of the first symptoms of scurvy, or vitamin C deficiency, is fatigue, so it is possible that the sick who were given these syrups were cured of what ailed them.

Red currants are also high in pectin and so are frequently combined with other, lower pectin fruits, such as raspberries and apricots, to make jams and jellies more spreadable. This combination of raspberries and red currants is a favorite of mine. It is best to use red currant purée rather than the whole fruit because both red currants and raspberries are quite seedy.

2 pints (448 g) red currants, de-stemmed
½ cup (120 ml) water
2 pints (500 g) red raspberries
3 cups (600 g) sugar

Finding Red Currants

Red currants turn from white to a glossy ruby-red and are ready to pick in early July. It can be hard to find these members of the Ribes family. When you do find them, usually at farmers' markets, they can be shockingly expensive. Nevertheless, it is worth splurging on a few pints every year if only to make this exquisite jam. Or perhaps you can find a source to pick your own. I pick red currants from a friend's backyard shrubs; she lets me pick the entire crop in exchange for a jar or two of jam.

▶▶▶ MAKES FOUR 8-OUNCE (235 ML) JARS ◀◀◀

Prepare a boiling water bath and heat four 8-ounce (235 ml) jars. Place a saucer in the freezer to chill.

Combine the currants and the water in a large saucepan. Bring to a boil over high heat. Turn down the heat and simmer until the currants have burst, about 5 minutes. Mash them a bit with a potato masher.

Strain the currant mixture through a fine-mesh sieve into a large bowl. Stir and press down on the fruit to extract as much pulp and juice as possible, leaving behind only the seeds and skin. Measure the red currant purée and discard the solids. You should have between 1½ and 2 cups (345 to 460 g).

Return the purée to the saucepan and add the raspberries. Crush the raspberries with a potato masher. Add the sugar and bring the mixture to a boil over high heat. Turn the heat down to medium-high. Boil the jam, stirring constantly, for 10 to 12 minutes.

Remove the saucer from the freezer and place a dollop of jam on it. Return it to the freezer for 1 minute. Remove the saucer and push the dollop of jam with your finger. If it wrinkles, then the jam is set. If not, continue to cook the jam and try the test again after a few minutes.

Remove the jam from the heat and skim off any foam. Ladle the jam into the jars, leaving ¼ inch (6 mm) of headspace at the top. Bubble the jars and wipe the rims with a damp cloth. Place the lids on the jars and screw on the rings just until you feel resistance. Process the jars in a boiling water bath for 10 minutes. Allow to cool in the water for 5 minutes before removing. Store in a cool, dark place for up to 1 year.

ROSE PETAL SYRUP

Rose-flavored beverages, ice cream, and other sweets, including Turkish delight, are common throughout the Middle East, the Levant, and India. In the Sephardic world, rose-flavored dishes are traditional for Shavuot, which is known as the Feast of the Roses because of the custom of decorating the synagogue with rose petals for the holiday.

Use this stunning pink syrup to flavor beverages, whipped cream, or homemade ice cream. It is also delicious drizzled on pound cake or the Egyptian Semolina Cake on page 148.

Make sure to source organic, unsprayed rose petals to use in cooking. The more fragrant the flowers, the stronger the flavor. For a beautiful deep red or pink syrup, choose healthy, brightly colored petals and use them soon after harvesting.

2 cups (32 g) loosely packed
*   rose petals*
1½ cups (355 ml) water
2 cups (400 g) sugar
2 teaspoons freshly squeezed
*   lemon juice*
Rose water (if needed)

➤➤➤ MAKES 1 PINT (475 ML) ◄◄◄

Place the rose petals in a heatproof glass bowl. Bring the water to a boil and pour it over the rose petals. Cover and allow to steep for at least 2 hours.

Squeeze the petals to extract as much liquid as possible.

Strain out the petals and any seeds and pour the liquid into a medium saucepan. It should be red or pink in color. Add the sugar and heat over medium heat, stirring to dissolve the sugar.

Increase the heat to high and bring to a boil. Boil for 5 minutes.

Remove from the heat and add the lemon juice. If your rose petals did not infuse the syrup with enough of a rose flavor, you can also add ¼ to ½ teaspoon of rose water, but use caution. Too much rose water will make your syrup taste like soap or perfume. Pour the syrup into a clean and sterilized pint (475 ml) jar and store in the refrigerator for several months.

SHTETL RASPBERRY SYRUP

Raspberry syrup is a beautiful, delicious concoction that is perfect for flavoring lemonade, iced tea, or that traditional Jewish favorite, seltzer. You can also use raspberry syrup to make elegant and festive cocktails. And it has many uses beyond beverages: Use it as a topping for ice cream or yogurt. Pour it on your breakfast pancakes and waffles. Or transform a simple pound cake into a dessert fit for company.

In the past, raspberry syrup was far more than something to mix into your drink or enjoy on your dessert. Claudia Roden writes in *The Book of Jewish Food* that it was given as a tonic to the sick in the shtetls of eastern Europe and Russia. There is a first-hand account of this practice in the memoir of Bernard Abrahams, a Lithuanian Jew born in 1880 who emigrated first to South Africa before settling in Israel. In *Mayne zibetsik yor*, Abrahams writes: "Blueberries and red raspberries grew abundantly in the nearby forests. On the long summer days, the villagers would hike into the forests and pick to their hearts' content. From the berries they would cook all sorts of soups and syrups for winter, to be used by the ill and feeble."

Although we have more effective cures today, I like the idea of preserving the flavor and color of raspberries at their peak—in late summer and fall—and enjoying their goodness all year long. Who knows, maybe a dose of raspberry syrup will help you beat that winter cold!

*4 pints (about 9 cups, or 1.1 kg)
   raspberries*
2 cups (475 ml) water
4 cups (800 g) sugar
*3 tablespoons (45 ml) freshly
   squeezed lemon juice*

➤➤➤ MAKES FIVE 8-OUNCE (235 ML) JARS ◀◀◀

Prepare a boiling water bath and heat five 8-ounce (235 ml) jars.

Combine the raspberries and water in a large saucepan. Bring to a boil over high heat, mashing the berries with a potato masher or fork. Simmer the berries for 5 minutes until broken down.

Strain the mixture through a fine-mesh sieve into a large bowl. Stir the pulp in the sieve to extract as much juice as possible. You can also leave the pulp in the sieve for an hour to allow more liquid to drain. Measure the raspberry juice; you should have approximately 1 quart (950 ml).

Return the juice to the saucepan. Add the sugar and lemon juice. Bring the mixture to a boil over high heat, stirring to dissolve the sugar. Boil hard for 1 minute.

Remove the syrup from the heat and skim off any foam that has accumulated. Ladle the syrup into the jars, leaving ½ inch (1 cm) of headspace. Bubble the jars and wipe the rims with a damp cloth. Skim off any foam on the top of the syrup. Place the lids on the jars and screw on the rings just until you feel resistance. Process the jars in a boiling water bath for 10 minutes. Allow to cool in the water for 5 minutes before removing. Store in a cool, dark place for up to 1 year.

RASPBERRY SYRUP: A TONIC FOR THE SICK

Why did Jews in the shtetl view raspberry syrup as having medicinal properties? To be sure, raspberries are high in vitamin C and act as an anti-inflammatory. As a result, raspberry syrup may have actually helped to heal some of the people that were dosed with it, depending on the nature of their complaints.

Before modern medicine, raspberry syrup was held in such high esteem as a cure because red foods, such as raspberries, were believed to aid the body in weaknesses related to the heart or to blood, which, of course, is also red. Indeed, William Harvey, who discovered the circulation of the blood in 1626, stated that: "From consideration of the colouring of each thing comes the knowledge of the degree of its kinship to blood, its temperament and active movement." Thus, raspberry syrup, with its bright red color, also would have been used to strengthen a weak person by fortifying his or her blood.

BLACK CURRANT SYRUP

As one might guess from their inky blue-black hue, black currants are packed with nutrients, including vitamins C and A, iron, potassium, magnesium, zinc, folic acid, and flavonoids. Black currants have been shown to act as an anti-inflammatory and to fight infection. Long before they knew about vitamins, minerals, and antioxidants, Jews in eastern Europe knew that foods had medicinal properties, and they used them in all sorts of folk cures, from fevers to gout to arthritis. Even the leaves, bark, and roots of the black currant bush were mashed and boiled to make folk remedies.

This syrup is delicious mixed with seltzer or as an ingredient in cocktails. With its high concentration of vitamin C, it also is a surprisingly effective remedy for colds, sore throats, and coughs. Polish and Russian Jews used it for that purpose for centuries. Look for black currants at farmers' markets in June and July. If you are unable to find black currants near you, you can order frozen berries or concentrate online.

3 pints black currants (about 2½ pounds, or 1 kg), stems removed
2½ cups (570 ml) water
⅓ cup (80 ml) freshly squeezed lemon juice
2 cups (400 g) sugar

▸▸▸ MAKES THREE 8-OUNCE (235 ML) JARS ◂◂◂

Combine the black currants and water in a medium saucepan and bring to a boil over high heat. Turn down the heat and simmer, uncovered, until the currants begin to break down, about 10 minutes. Crush the currants with a fork or potato masher.

Place the currants in a fine-mesh sieve lined with cheesecloth set over a large bowl. Allow to drain for at least 6 hours and preferably overnight. Press down on or squeeze the currants to extract as much juice as possible. Discard the solids.

Prepare a boiling water bath and heat three 8-ounce (235 ml) jars.

Measure the black currant juice. You should have about 2 cups (475 ml). Combine the black currant juice, lemon juice, and sugar in a medium saucepan and bring to a boil. Boil the mixture hard for 1 minute. Skim off any foam that has accumulated.

Ladle the syrup into the clean, warm jars, leaving ¼ inch (6 mm) of headspace at the top. Bubble the jars and wipe the rims with a damp cloth. If any foam or bubbles appear on the top of the syrup, skim that off and wipe the lids again. Place the lids on the jars and screw on the rings just until you feel resistance. Process the jars in a boiling water bath for 10 minutes. Allow to cool in the water for 5 minutes before removing. Store in a cool, dark place for up to 1 year.

Jews and Seltzer

You can mix any of the syrups in this book with carbonated water—whether you call it seltzer, club soda, or soda water—for a refreshing and brightly colored beverage. Seltzer is a particular form of carbonated water that, unlike club soda, does not contain salt. In the United States, seltzer is so closely associated with Jewish people that it used to be known as Jewish champagne.

The name seltzer comes from the German town of Niederselters, which began producing a naturally carbonated mineral water during the Renaissance. It was sold as a health tonic. In the nineteenth century, the technology for sealing carbonated water in bottles as well as the soda siphon were invented, creating the modern carbonated beverage industry.

Sparkling water, which could be flavored with syrup, was a useful beverage for Jews observing the kosher laws, who could not drink milk with meat meals. Many Jews in eastern Europe and Russia entered the seltzer business. When Jews began emigrating in large numbers to the United States, they brought the industry with them. Soon there was a new fixture of city life—the seltzer man, who every week delivered the green and blue siphon bottles (sometimes decorated with stars of David).

Until the 1950s, the neighborhood candy store was the center of communal life in New York. You could order a plain seltzer for two cents or a flavored one for three cents. Better yet, you could order an egg cream, which combined chocolate syrup, milk, and seltzer. After the Second World War, the role of seltzer diminished as sweetened carbonated beverages, like Coca-Cola (which finally became kosher in the 1950s), gained favor.

Today, with the popularity of home water-carbonation machines, we are in a new golden age of sparkling water, and, along with it, there is a renewed interest in homemade drink syrups.

BLACK CURRANT JAM

Black currants have a complex, slightly musky taste and aroma. They are native to northern Europe and Siberia, where they thrive during the long, cold winters. Although they are beloved in Europe, Americans are even less familiar with black currants than they are with red currants. Perhaps you have experienced their unique flavor in the French black currant liqueur, crème de cassis, which when mixed with white wine makes a delicious aperitif called a *kir*. Crème de cassis mixed with champagne is even more delicious and known as a *kir royale*.

Black currants are a gift to jam makers because they naturally contain just the right amounts of pectin and acidity. Because black currants are so tart, this jam contains equal amounts fruit and sugar. The water is necessary to ensure that the final product is not too thick. Because black currants are so high in pectin, be careful not to overcook your jam or you will end up with a final product that is too firm to spread.

**1 pound black currants
(about 1½ pints, or 455 g),
stems removed**
1 cup (235 ml) water
2 cups (400 g) sugar
Squeeze of fresh lemon juice

▶▶▶ MAKES TWO TO THREE 8-OUNCE (235 ML) JARS ◀◀◀

Prepare a boiling water bath and heat three 8-ounce (235 ml) jars. Place a saucer in the freezer to chill.

Combine the currants and water in a large saucepan. Bring to a boil over high heat. Turn down the heat and simmer until the currants have burst and begin to break down, about 5 to 7 minutes. Add the sugar and lemon juice and cook, stirring, over medium heat until the sugar dissolves. Raise the heat to high and bring the mixture to a boil. Boil the jam, stirring constantly, until it reaches 220°F (104°C) on a candy thermometer, about 5 to 7 minutes.

Remove the saucer from the freezer and place a dollop of jam on it. Return it to the freezer for 1 minute. Remove the saucer and push the dollop of jam with your finger. If it wrinkles, then the jam is set. If not, continue to cook the jam and try the test again after a few minutes.

Remove the jam from the heat and skim off any foam that has accumulated. Ladle the jam into the clean, warm jars, leaving ¼ inch (6 mm) of headspace at the top. Bubble the jars and wipe the rims with a damp cloth. Place the lids on the jars and screw on the rings just until you feel resistance. Process the jars in a boiling water bath for 10 minutes. Allow to cool in the water for 5 minutes before removing. Store in a cool, dark place for up to 1 year.

QUEEN ESTHER'S APRICOT-POPPY SEED JAM

Although not a traditional combination for jam, apricot and poppy seed are both traditional Purim foods. There are different stories about why Jews eat dishes containing poppy seeds at Purim. One poetic story is that Queen Esther subsisted on them during a three-day fast while she prayed to God to repeal Haman's murderous decree. Another is that when Queen Esther was living in the court of the Persian king and hiding her Jewish faith, she ate a vegetarian diet of mostly nuts and seeds to avoid breaking the kosher laws.

Purim usually falls in March, before apricots come into season. I suggest preparing this jam in advance, when apricots are in season in June or July, and saving it for next Purim. It makes a wonderful filling for Hamentaschen (page 145) or an impressive addition to *michlach manot*.

**6 cups diced apricots
  (approximately 3 pounds,
  or 1.4 kg)
3½ cups (700 g) sugar
1 lemon
2 tablespoons (18 g) poppy seeds**

Michlach Manot

One of the central Purim rituals is *michlach manot*: sending gifts of food to friends and family.

There are a few rules about michlach manot: You are supposed to use a go-between to send gifts, not simply give them to the recipient. Also, the gift should include at least two different ready-to-eat foods.

Many of the recipes in this book would make charming Purim gifts, including Haman-taschen (page 145), which are a Purim must-have, and a special jar of your homemade jam.

»» MAKES THREE OR FOUR 8-OUNCE (235 ML) JARS ««

Prepare a boiling water bath and heat four 8-ounce (235 ml) jars. Place a saucer in the freezer to chill.

Combine the apricots and sugar in a large, deep saucepan. Heat over medium-high heat, stirring to dissolve the sugar. Bring the mixture to a boil, stirring constantly to prevent scorching. Boil until the fruit has broken down, about 10 minutes, stirring frequently. Add the zest and juice of the lemon and continue to boil.

When the jam appears thick and comes off a spoon in a sheet rather than in thin droplets, test for doneness. Remove the saucer from the freezer and place a dollop of jam on it. Return it to the freezer for 1 minute. Remove the saucer and push the dollop of jam with your finger. If it wrinkles, then the jam is set. If not, continue to cook the jam and try the test again after a few minutes.

Remove the jam from the heat and stir in the poppy seeds. Ladle the jam into the clean, warm jars, leaving ¼ inch (6 mm) of headspace at the top. Bubble the jars and wipe the rims with a damp cloth. Place the lids on the jars and screw on the rings just until you feel resistance. Process the jars in a boiling water bath for 10 minutes. Allow to cool in the water for 5 minutes before removing. Store in a cool, dark place for up to 1 year.

APRICOT WALNUT EINGEMACHT

Eingemacht is a Yiddish word for preserves or jams made with fruit—or even root vegetables, such as radishes or beets—cooked in honey or sugar. Eingemachts were traditionally served for special occasions, such as Passover, but when sugar became more affordable in the nineteenth century, they became commonplace. A proud Russian or Polish Jewish housewife would serve her home-made eingemachts to guests as an accompaniment to scalding hot tea or bring them to her hostess as a house gift.

This apricot walnut conserve is similar to a traditional eingemacht because it includes dried fruits and nuts in addition to fresh fruit. However, traditional eingemachts were more akin to what we now call preserves, with fruit and nuts suspended in thick syrup. This spread's texture is more similar to jam. It makes a wonderful filling for Hamantaschen (see recipe on page 145) or sponge cake. Or simply spread it on challah or buttered matzo.

4 cups (660 g) diced fresh apricots

3 cups (600 g) sugar

½ cup (65 g) diced dried apricots

½ cup (120 ml) orange juice

2 tablespoons (28 ml) freshly squeezed lemon juice

½ cup (60 g) diced walnuts

>>> MAKES FOUR 8-OUNCE (235 ML) JARS <<<

Prepare a boiling water bath and heat four 8-ounce (235 ml) jars. Place a saucer in the freezer to chill.

Combine the fresh apricots, sugar, dried apricots, orange juice, and lemon juice in a large saucepan. Bring the mixture to a boil over medium-high heat, stirring to dissolve the sugar.

Reduce the heat to medium and continue to boil for 10 minutes. Add the walnuts and boil for an additional 5 minutes.

Remove the pot from the heat. Remove the saucer from the freezer and place a dollop of jam on it. Return it to the freezer for 1 minute. Remove the saucer and push the dollop of jam with your finger. If it wrinkles, it is done. If not, return it to the heat, cook a few more minutes, and try the test again.

Ladle the jam into the clean, warm jars, leaving ¼ inch (6 mm) of headspace at the top. Bubble the jars and wipe the rims with a damp cloth. Place the lids on the jars and screw on the rings just until you feel resistance. Process the jars in a boiling water bath for 10 minutes. Allow to cool in the water for 5 minutes before removing. Store in a cool, dark place for up to 1 year.

APRICOTS IN HEAVY SYRUP (APRICOT SPOON SWEET)

Brought to Spain by the Arabs during the Middle Ages, apricots are among the most commonly preserved fruits in the Sephardic world. Following their expulsion from Spain, many Spanish Jews settled in Turkey, where apricots grew in abundance. Apricots, along with oranges and quince, became one of the fruits that Sephardic housewives turned into *dulces*, or spoon sweets, thick confections of fruit preserved in syrup.

In Turkey and the Middle East, Jewish hosts customarily offered visitors coffee and a spoonful of dulce, which was served from glass bowls on silver trays. These special household items were often part of a bride's dowry. A spoonful of dulce was also a common way to celebrate Shabbat. Following the death of a close relative, a mourner would refrain from taking dulce with his coffee for one year. After the mourning period ended, a neighbor would bring the mourner some of her home-made dulce to mark his or her reintegration into the everyday world.

I suggest we take a note from the cooks who invented these luscious sweets and enjoy them in moderation. A spoonful or two straight out of the jar is a perfect after-dinner treat. Or spoon a few apricots and some syrup over ice cream or pound cake to transform those humble foods into an elegant dessert. This recipe makes more syrup than you will likely need; it can be stored in the refrigerator and used to sweeten beverages.

3 pounds (1.4 kg) apricots
Juice of 1 lemon
5 cups (1 kg) sugar
5 cups (1.2 L) water

»»» MAKES 3 PINTS (1.4 L) «««

Wash, halve, and pit the apricots. Toss gently with the lemon juice to prevent them from browning. Set aside.

To make the syrup, combine the sugar and water in a large, wide pan such as a Dutch oven. Bring to a boil over high heat, stirring frequently. Then reduce the heat to medium-low and simmer for 5 minutes.

Add the apricots and any accumulated juices to the syrup, spooning them in carefully to keep the apricots in one layer. Simmer for 5 minutes, gently pushing the apricot halves to submerge them in the syrup, but taking care not to crush or mash the fruit. Turn off the heat and let the fruit and syrup cool. Refrigerate for twenty-four hours. The following day, prepare a boiling water bath and heat 3 pint (475 ml) jars. Using a slotted spoon, remove the apricots from the syrup and set them aside. Pour the syrup into the same low, wide pan and bring to a boil over high heat. Reduce the heat slightly and boil for 5 to 7 minutes. The temperature should register 210°F to 220°F (99°C to 104°C) on a candy thermometer. Skim off any foam or scum that accumulates.

When the syrup has reduced by one-third to one-half, carefully add the apricots in one layer and heat them through. Divide the fruit among the three jars, taking care not to crush or damage it. Ladle the syrup over the fruit in the jars, leaving ½ inch (1 cm) of headspace at the top. Bubble the jars and wipe the rims with a damp cloth. Place the lids on the jars and screw on the rings just until you feel resistance. Process the jars in a boiling water bath for 20 minutes. Allow to cool in the water for 5 minutes before removing. Store in a cool, dark place for up to 1 year.

Note: It is inevitable that the fruit will float to the top of the jars. Do not be concerned. Packing the fruit as tightly as possible will minimize "fruit float."

APRICOT-ORANGE BLOSSOM JAM

Apricots are a low-acid and low-pectin fruit, so this jam has a soft set. It has the looser texture typical of Sephardic jams, which were traditionally eaten straight out of the jar or stirred into yogurt, rather than spread onto bread as jam is in the Western world. Using barely ripe or even underripe apricots will ensure that the final product is more jam than syrup.

Orange blossom water is a distillation of the flowers of the bitter orange tree. It is a common flavoring in Middle Eastern, North African, Persian, and Turkish cuisines, and it is a symbol of good fortune in the Jewish communities from these regions. You can find it at Middle Eastern grocers and spice stores or online. Its delicate floral taste makes it an intriguing and unusual addition to pastries, desserts, and even cocktails.

8 cups sliced, pitted apricots (approximately 3 pounds, or 1.4 kg)
4 cups (800 g) sugar
Zest and juice of 1 lemon
1 tablespoon (15 ml) orange blossom water

»» MAKES FIVE OR SIX 8-OUNCE (235 ML) JARS ««

Combine the apricots, sugar, and lemon zest and juice in a large bowl and stir gently to combine. Cover and refrigerate overnight, stirring occasionally to distribute the sugar. The result will be slightly shriveled slices of fruit in a thick syrup. Stir to dissolve any remaining sugar.

The following day, prepare a boiling water bath and heat six 8-ounce (235 ml) jars. Place a saucer in the freezer to chill.

Drain the fruit, reserving the syrup. Place the syrup in a large, deep saucepan. The jam will foam and bubble dramatically as it cooks, so be certain to use a large pot. Bring to a boil over medium-high heat. Add the fruit and return to a boil. Stirring constantly to prevent scorching, boil the jam hard for 10 to 15 minutes.

When the fruit has broken down, remove the saucer from the freezer and place a dollop of jam on it. Return it to the freezer for 1 minute. Remove the saucer and push the dollop of jam with your finger. If it wrinkles, then the jam is set. If not, continue to cook the jam and try the test again after a few minutes.

Remove the jam from the heat and allow the boiling to subside. Stir in the orange blossom water. Skim off any foam that has accumulated. Ladle the jam into the clean, warm jars, leaving ¼ inch (6 mm) of headspace at the top. If there are burned or caramelized bits on the bottom of the pan, avoid those. Bubble the jars and wipe the rims with a damp cloth. Place the lids on the jars and screw on the rings just until you feel resistance. Process the jars in a boiling water bath for 10 minutes. Allow to cool in the water for 5 minutes before removing. Store in a cool, dark place for up to one year.

GOOSEBERRY JAM

Gooseberries are beloved in Europe, but unfamiliar to most Americans. There is a straightforward explanation for this. In the early 1900s, the U.S. government banned the cultivation of currants and gooseberries, which belong to the same genus, under the belief that they hosted a disease that infected pine trees. The ban was only lifted in the 1960s.

Native to northern Europe, gooseberries flourish in cooler climes. Although the fruit is most commonly associated with British cuisine, gooseberries grow abundantly in Germany, Holland, the Czech Republic, Poland, and Scandinavia. Before people in northern countries had easy access to the citrus fruits grown in southern Europe, gooseberries and currants were used to add tartness to cooked dishes. Gooseberries even pop up in savory foods, such as *bigos*, a Polish meat stew.

Gooseberries are naturally high in pectin, making them ideal for jam and jelly. Despite the absence of added pectin, this is a jam with a firm set. A good source of vitamin C, gooseberries would no doubt have been preserved by Polish Jews, as well as their Gentile neighbors, to last through the long winter. Unlike most berries, gooseberries are relatively hardy, and they will last for a week or more in the refrigerator after picking.

2 pints (600 g) gooseberries
1 cup (235 ml) water
2 tablespoons (28 ml) lemon juice
3 cups (600 g) sugar

▶▶▶ MAKES THREE 8-OUNCE (235 ML) JARS ◀◀◀

Prepare a boiling water bath and heat three 8-ounce (235 ml) jars. Place a saucer in the freezer to chill.

Remove the stems and blossom ends from the gooseberries, a process known as topping and tailing the berries. The easiest way to do this is with kitchen shears.

Combine the gooseberries, water, and lemon juice in a large saucepan. Bring to a boil over high heat and then turn down the heat and simmer until the berries break down, about 15 minutes. Add the sugar all at once and return to a boil, stirring to dissolve the sugar. Boil the jam hard for 10 minutes, stirring frequently to prevent scorching.

Remove the saucer from the freezer and place a dollop of jam on it. Return it to the freezer for 1 minute. Remove the saucer and push the dollop of jam with your finger. If it wrinkles, then the jam is set. If not, continue to cook the jam and try the test again after a few minutes.

Remove the jam from the heat and skim off any foam. Ladle the jam into the jars, leaving ¼ inch (6 mm) of headspace. Bubble the jars and wipe the rims with a damp cloth. Place the lids on the jars and screw on the rings just until you feel resistance. Process the jars in a boiling water bath for 10 minutes. Allow to cool in the water for 5 minutes before removing. Store in a cool, dark place for up to 1 year.

SOUR CHERRY AND ALMOND CONSERVE

In eastern Europe, Jewish cooks often added chopped bitter almonds to their homemade jams, particularly plum, berry, and cherry. Bitter almonds have a strong and unique flavor that is different from the sweet almonds we eat today. Raw, bitter almonds contain a form of cyanide and thus can be dangerous to consume. (The cyanide evaporates when cooked, so none of the wives and mothers back in the shtetl were poisoning their families.) Nevertheless, it remains illegal to sell bitter almonds in the United States, although not in Europe where bitter almond is used to flavor pastries, candies, and liqueurs. This recipe is inspired by those traditional Ashkenazi jams incorporating bitter almond, but it uses safe, sweet almonds instead.

Almonds are a symbol of good luck and fruitfulness for the Jewish people, and they are used in many traditional Ashkenazi and Sephardic dishes, including many kinds of charoset.

3 pounds (1.4 kg) frozen sour cherries, thawed

1 cup (235 ml) juice from the thawed cherries

2 cups (400 g) sugar

¼ cup (60 ml) lemon juice

¼ cup (28 g) slivered blanched almonds

¼ teaspoon ground allspice

▶▶▶ MAKES THREE 8-OUNCE (235 ML) JARS ◀◀◀

Prepare a boiling water bath and heat three 8-ounce (235 ml) jars. Place a saucer in the freezer to chill.

Combine the cherries, cherry juice, sugar, and lemon juice in a large, deep saucepan. Heat over medium heat, stirring to dissolve the sugar. Raise the heat to medium-high and bring to a boil. Boil, stirring frequently, until the liquid is thick and syrupy and the cherries have shrunk and become wizened, about 30 minutes. Lower the heat to medium as needed to prevent scorching.

Remove the saucer from the freezer and place several cherries and spoonful of syrup on it. Return it to the freezer for 1 minute. Remove the saucer and push the syrup with your finger. If it wrinkles, then the conserve is set. If not, continue to cook and try the test again after a few minutes. Remove the pot from the heat and add the almonds and allspice.

Ladle the conserve into the clean, warm jars, taking care to distribute the almonds evenly, leaving ¼ inch (6 mm) of headspace at the top. Bubble the jars and wipe the rims with a damp cloth.

Place the lids on the jars and screw on the rings just until you feel resistance. Process the jars in a boiling water bath for 10 minutes. Allow to cool in the water for 5 minutes before removing. Store in a cool, dark place for up to 1 year.

RUSSIAN-STYLE SOUR CHERRY PRESERVES

Cherries are an ancient fruit but unlike many other ancient fruits, do not appear anywhere in the Bible or Talmud. Nevertheless, as cherries grow abundantly throughout Europe and the Middle East, they are a vital part of both Ashkenazi and Sephardic Jewish cuisines.

There are two kinds of cherries: sweet and sour. Sweet cherries can be eaten fresh. Sour cherries, which are smaller and less shiny, are primarily used for baking, preserving, and juice. I find that most sweet cherries, while delicious for eating out of hand, can be cloying as a jam, so I use sour cherries for preserving. Sour cherries are notoriously fragile and perishable, and they are not usually sold in grocery stores. You may have to seek them out at a local farmers' market during their relatively short season, but it is worth the effort.

This kind of cherry preserve, with whole fruits suspended in syrup, is typical of Russian cuisine. The fruit preserves are not spread on bread or toast, but rather eaten with a spoon to accompany tea. You may enjoy these cherries over ice cream, as a topping for cheese blintzes, or swirled into yogurt.

2 pounds (910 g) sour cherries, pitted
2 cups (400 g) sugar
2 tablespoons (28 ml) lemon juice
¼ teaspoon cinnamon
⅛ teaspoon ground cloves

»» MAKES THREE 8-OUNCE (235 ML) JARS ««

Prepare a boiling water bath and heat three 8-ounce (235 ml) jars.

Combine the cherries, sugar, and lemon juice in a large pot. Let it sit for an hour until the cherries have released their juices and the sugar has mostly dissolved. If using frozen cherries, thaw them completely before continuing.

Stir the fruit and collected juices. Add the cinnamon and cloves and bring the mixture to a boil over high heat. Reduce the heat to medium-low and simmer until the liquid has reduced by half, about 20 minutes. It may seem watery, but it will thicken as it cools.

Ladle an even amount of cherries and syrup into the clean, warm jars, leaving ½ inch (1 cm) of headspace at the top. Bubble the jars well, adding more syrup if necessary, and wipe the rims with a damp cloth. Place the lids on the jars and screw on the rings just until you feel resistance.

Process the jars in a boiling water bath for 10 minutes. Allow to cool in the water for 5 minutes before removing. Store in a cool, dark place for up to 1 year.

Note: You may have leftover syrup. Save it to flavor seltzer or cocktails.

ALSATIAN BRANDIED SOUR CHERRIES

In the past, Ashkenazi Jews from France to Russia made spirits from sour cherries in part because cherries, unlike grapes, do not require any special supervision under the kosher laws when fermented into alcohol. This recipe combines sour cherries and brandy. It is inspired by the well-known cherry brandy, kirsch, which is part of the Jewish cuisine of Alsace and western Germany. Use these brandied cherries to garnish cocktails, especially Manhattans, or as a dessert topping.

Sour cherries freeze exceptionally well, so your enjoyment of them does not have to be limited to their short season. I recommend buying pitted cherries to freeze or, if you are more enterprising than I am, pit your own cherries before freezing. This recipe specifically calls for frozen cherries to make use of your freezer stash.

Use the tall, 12-ounce (355 ml) jars here for an especially attractive presentation.

1 cup (200 g) sugar

¾ cup (175 ml) water

1 teaspoon vanilla bean paste or
  ½ of a vanilla bean

2 tablespoons (28 ml) lemon juice

2 pounds (910 g) frozen sour
  cherries (pitted), unthawed

½ cup (120 ml) brandy

>>> MAKES THREE 12-OUNCE (355 ML) JARS <<<

Prepare a boiling water bath and heat three 12-ounce (355 ml) jars.

In a large saucepan over medium heat, combine the sugar, water, vanilla bean paste, and lemon juice. (If using a vanilla bean, slice the bean open lengthwise and scrape the interior into the pan. Then add the bean itself.) Stir to dissolve the sugar.

When the sugar is dissolved, reduce the heat to low and add the frozen cherries. Stir gently to coat them with the syrup and simmer over low heat until the cherries are thawed and release their juices, about 10 to 15 minutes. Raise the heat to medium and cook until the cherries and syrup are hot, stirring occasionally, about 10 more minutes. Remove from the heat. Add the brandy and stir to gently combine. Remove the vanilla bean (if using).

Fill the clean, warm jars with the cherries and syrup, leaving ½ inch (1 cm) of headspace. Bubble the jars well and add more cherries or syrup, as necessary, to maintain the headspace. Wipe the rims with a damp cloth. Place the lids on the jars and screw on the rings just until you feel resistance.

Process the jars in a boiling water bath for 10 minutes. Allow to cool in the water for 5 minutes before removing. Store in a cool, dark place for up to 1 year.

Note: I recommend vanilla bean paste or a vanilla bean in this recipe instead of vanilla extract because of the high heat and long cooking time.

MULBERRY JAM

Mulberries were one of the most important berries for people of the ancient Mediterranean and were consumed by the Jews in Israel during Biblical times. Sephardic Jews from the Middle East and the Levant incorporated mulberries into their cuisine, using them to make syrup, jam, or fruit paste. Mulberries remain a popular fruit for eating and preserving in the eastern Mediterranean today.

Most Americans, however, are not familiar with fresh mulberries or, at least, they are not familiar with them as a fruit to eat. Soft and fragile, fresh mulberries are nearly impossible to find in stores or even farmers' markets. There are mulberry trees all over the country. But the fruits are difficult to harvest because the trees are tall and the berries do not ripen at the same time.

The best way to harvest mulberries is to lay a clean sheet or tarp under the tree and then shake the branches. The ripe berries will fall to the ground. Their taste is similar to that of a blackberry but sweeter and less juicy. If you can forage mulberries from a tree in your area when they ripen in early summer, I encourage you to do so and give mulberry jam a try. It's a clever way to get something for nothing.

1 quart (560 g) mulberries
1⅓ cups (266 g) sugar
Juice of ½ of a lemon

▶▶▶ MAKES TWO 8-OUNCE (235 ML) JARS ◀◀◀

Prepare a boiling water bath and heat two 8-ounce (235 ml) jars. Place a saucer in the freezer to chill.

Place a layer of berries in the bottom of a bowl and gently mash with the tines of a fork. Repeat, adding berries one layer at a time, until all the berries are mashed.

Combine the mashed berries, sugar, and lemon juice in a large deep saucepan or Dutch oven. Heat over medium heat, stirring frequently, until the sugar dissolves. Increase the heat to high and bring the mixture to a boil. Reduce the heat and simmer, stirring frequently to prevent scorching, until the jam is thickened, about 12 to 15 minutes.

Take the jam off the heat. Remove the saucer from the freezer and place a spoonful of jam on it. Return it to the freezer for 1 minute. Remove it and push the jam with your finger. If it wrinkles, then it is set. If not, continue to cook and try the test again after a few minutes.

Ladle the jam into the clean, warm jars, leaving ¼ inch (6 mm) of headspace at the top. Bubble the jars and wipe the rims with a damp cloth. Place the lids on the jars and screw on the rings just until you feel resistance. Process the jars in a boiling water bath for 10 minutes. Allow to cool in the water for 5 minutes before removing. Store in a cool, dark place for up to 1 year.

FAUX MULBERRY JAM (BLUEBERRY AND BLACKBERRY JAM)

If you cannot find mulberries to harvest near you or are wary of eating the ones you do find, this combination of blueberries and blackberries mimics the sweet-tart taste of the mulberry as well as its deep, purple color. This faux mulberry jam is popular with everyone, especially children, and is lovely spread on challah.

2½ cups (363 g) blackberries
    (1 heaping pint)
2½ cups (363 g) blueberries
    (1 heaping pint)
1¾ cups (350 g) sugar
    (approximately)
2 tablespoons (28 ml) lemon juice
Zest of 1 lemon
½ teaspoon ground ginger

▶▶▶ MAKES THREE 8-OUNCE (235 ML) JARS ◀◀◀

Prepare a boiling water bath and heat three 8-ounce (235 ml) jars. Place a saucer in the freezer to chill.

Place a layer of berries in the bottom of a bowl and gently mash with the tines of a fork. Repeat, adding berries one layer at a time, until all the berries are mashed. Measure the mashed berries and then pour them into a large pot or Dutch oven.

Divide the amount of mashed berries in half and add that amount of sugar to the pot. (For example, if you end up with 3½ cups [700 g] of mashed berries, use 1¾ cups [350 g] of sugar.)

Stir the berries and sugar together in the pot and let sit for 20 to 30 minutes so that the mixture becomes juicy and the sugar dissolves.

Add the lemon juice, zest, and ginger and stir well. Bring to a boil over medium-high heat. Reduce the heat slightly and continue cooking, stirring frequently to prevent scorching, until the berry mixture reaches 220°F (104°C) on a candy thermometer, about 20 minutes. Skim off any foam that has accumulated.

Remove the saucer from the freezer and place a spoonful of jam on it. Return it to the freezer for 1 minute. Remove the saucer and push the jam with your finger. If it wrinkles, then the jam is set. If not, continue to cook and try the test again after a few minutes.

Ladle the jam into the clean, warm jars, leaving ¼ inch (6 mm) of headspace at the top. Bubble the jars and wipe the rims with a damp cloth. Place the lids on the jars and screw on the rings just until you feel resistance. Process the jars in a boiling water bath for 10 minutes. Allow to cool in the water for 5 minutes before removing. Store in a cool, dark place for up to 1 year.

SWEET AND SOUR PEACH KETCHUP

The idea that ketchup is made with tomatoes is a fairly recent innovation. Ketchup, which is no more than a slow-simmered sauce made with fruit, vinegar, and spices, had a storied history in Asia and Europe long before the people of those continents encountered tomatoes, which are, after all, a New World crop.

The combination of sweet and sour flavors, such as ketchup's combination of fruit and vinegar, is a hallmark of Ashkenazi cuisine. Gil Marks notes in the *Encyclopedia of Jewish Food* that preparing dishes ahead of time to serve on Shabbat, in keeping with the prohibition against kindling a fire on the holiday, led Jewish cooks to rely on vinegar as a preservative. Sweet flavors were then added to cut the sharpness of the vinegar.

For centuries, Jewish cooks made ketchups of all kinds with the fruits and vegetables available to them. Here I have updated the tradition to create a peach ketchup. The sweet, tangy flavor of this ketchup is outstanding on turkey burgers and chicken sandwiches. My family also enjoys it on sweet potato fries.

5 pounds (2.3 kg) yellow peaches, peeled and diced
1 yellow onion, diced
3 cloves of garlic, minced
2 cups (475 ml) apple cider vinegar
1½ cups (340 g) brown sugar
1 tablespoon (18 g) pickling salt
1 teaspoon ground cloves
½ teaspoon nutmeg
Pinch of cayenne pepper

▶▶▶ MAKES FIVE OR SIX 8-OUNCE (235 ML) JARS ◀◀◀

Prepare a boiling water bath and heat six 8-ounce (235 ml) jars.

Combine all of the ingredients in a large saucepan and bring to a boil over high heat. Turn the heat down and simmer until the peaches are soft, about 10 minutes. Purée the mixture using an immersion blender or in batches in a food processor.

Return the mixture to a boil, reduce the heat again, and simmer until the ketchup is thick, spreadable, and will mound up on a spoon, about 1 to 1½ hours.

Ladle the ketchup into the clean, warm jars, leaving ½ inch (1 cm) of headspace at the top. Bubble the jars and wipe the rims with a damp cloth. Place the lids on the jars and screw on the rings just until you feel resistance. Process the jars in a boiling water bath for 15 minutes. Allow to cool in the water for 5 minutes before removing. Store in a cool, dark place for up to 1 year.

PEACHES IN HONEY SYRUP

Honey was the most important sweetener for Europeans until the eighteenth century when the Caribbean became home to large numbers of sugar plantations. Even then, sugar remained an expensive luxury item for most until the emergence of European sugar beet refineries in the nineteenth century. Thus, honey-sweetened side dishes, such as tzimmes, and desserts, such as honey cake, are common in Ashkenazi cuisine. Honey is a traditional food for Rosh Hashanah and is used to symbolize the hope that the coming year will be a sweet one.

Honey adds both sweetness and flavor to these preserved peach halves. These peaches would be delicious over ice cream or cake, but they are very satisfying on their own with a dollop of Greek yogurt or crème fraîche. The leftover syrup can be used to sweeten beverages or glaze a cake. A note: do not waste your expensive raw honey on this project because the heat from the boiling water bath will destroy the beneficial antioxidants and subtle flavor.

8 pounds (3.6 kg) peaches

Juice of 1 lemon

4 cups (950 ml) water

1½ cups (300 g) sugar

1½ cups (510 g) honey

8 cinnamon sticks

8 whole cloves

8 whole allspice berries

»» MAKES 4 QUARTS (3.8 L) ««

Prepare a boiling water bath and heat 4 quart (950 ml) jars. Do not cover the jars completely with water, otherwise the water level will be too high when you return the filled jars to the pot.

Peel and halve the peaches, removing the stone. Take care to keep the peach halves intact. Save any that break for another use.

Place the peach halves in a large bowl and spritz with lemon juice to keep them from browning.

In a large saucepan, combine the water, sugar, and honey. Bring the mixture to a boil over medium-high heat, stirring to dissolve the sugar, and then remove.

Working quickly, remove one of the jars from the water bath and fill it with peach halves, packing the fruit in as tightly as possible without damaging it. Place 2 cinnamon sticks, 2 whole cloves, and 2 allspice berries in the jar. Repeat with the remaining 3 jars.

Ladle the syrup over the fruit, leaving 1 inch (2.5 cm) of headspace at the top. Bubble the jars and wipe the rims with a damp cloth. Place the lids on the jars and screw on the rings just until you feel resistance. Process the jars in a boiling water bath for 25 minutes, making sure that the water covers the jars. (The jars will siphon quite a bit.) Allow to cool in the water for 5 minutes before removing. Store in a cool, dark place for up to 1 year.

SLOW COOKER PEACH LEKVAR (PEACH BUTTER)

According to the *Encyclopedia of Jewish Food*, fruit butter was traditionally made by boiling fruit outdoors over an open fire for hours, with people taking turns stirring the kettle. The fruit butter could then be stored in crocks to last through winter. In Europe, the most common fruit butter was made with plums, but apricots, apples, and peaches were also preserved in the same way.

Think of the slow cooker as the modern-day equivalent of that outdoor kettle. Peach butter still takes hours to cook down to the desired consistency, but at least with a slow cooker almost all of that time is passive. You will be delighted with how easy this project is, and the results are heavenly.

6 pounds (2.7 kg) peaches, peeled and pitted

3 cups (600 g) sugar

Juice of 1 lemon

▶▶▶ MAKES SIX 8-OUNCE (235 ML) JARS ◀◀◀

Purée the peaches in a food processor by pulsing several times, but stop when they are still chunky and not liquified. Add the purée and sugar to the bowl of the slow cooker.

Set the slow cooker to high and prop the lid open with the handle of a wooden spoon to allow for evaporation.

Cook the peach butter until it is dark, thick, and spreadable, checking it frequently. Occasionally, scrape down the sides and stir the mixture with the wooden spoon. The cooking process should take 6 to 8 hours, depending on the size of your slow cooker and the moisture level of the fruit.

When your fruit butter is close to done, prepare a boiling water bath and heat six 8-ounce (235 ml) jars. When you have achieved the texture you want, add the lemon juice and stir to combine.

Ladle peach butter into the jars, leaving ½ inch (1 cm) of headspace at the top. Bubble the jars and wipe the rims with a damp cloth. Place the lids on the jars and screw on the rings just until you feel resistance. Process the jars in a boiling water bath for 15 minutes. Allow to cool in the water for 5 minutes before removing. Store in a cool, dark place for up to 6 months.*

Note: If you do not have a slow cooker, make this recipe in a deep, wide saucepan or Dutch oven. It will take much less time, but will require more involvement on your part. To make peach butter in a regular pot, bring the mixture to a boil. Reduce the heat to low and simmer, stirring frequently to prevent scorching, until thick and concentrated. This could take up to two hours.

*Because fruit butters contain less sugar than jams, they have a shorter shelf life.

SUMMER TO FALL PEACH-FIG JAM

This jam symbolizes the transition from summer to fall with a combination of ancient and revered fruits. Figs are one of the Seven Species eaten by Jews in the land of Israel during Biblical times, and peaches are one of the new fruits mentioned in the Talmud.

Peaches leave the farmers' market just as fresh figs begin to appear in stores. With luck, there will be a brief period where the two overlap, perhaps right around Rosh Hashanah. Indeed, both figs and peaches are traditional Rosh Hashanah foods for many Sephardic communities. Capture that magical moment with this luscious, honey-scented jam. When you open a bottle in the dead of winter, you will be glad you did. Perhaps you will be reminded of your hopes and wishes for the new year and reflect on whether they have come to fruition.

1 pound (about 1 overflowing pint, or 455 g) figs, stemmed and diced

1 pound (about 3 large, or 455 g) peeled and diced yellow peaches

3 tablespoons (45 ml) lemon juice

1½ cups (300 g) sugar

1 cup (340 g) honey

½ teaspoon cinnamon

>>> MAKES FOUR 8-OUNCE (235 ML) JARS <<<

Prepare a boiling water bath and heat four 8-ounce (235 ml) jars. Place a saucer in the freezer to chill.

Place the figs, peaches, lemon juice, sugar, and honey in a wide, deep saucepan. Slowly bring to a boil over medium heat, stirring to dissolve the sugar. If the pieces of peach are large, crush them slightly with a potato masher to help them break down. Boil, stirring frequently to prevent scorching, until the jam thickens and fruit breaks down, about 15 minutes.

Remove the saucer from the freezer and place a dollop of jam on it. Return it to the freezer for 1 minute. Remove the saucer and push the dollop of jam with your finger. If it wrinkles, then the jam is set. If not, continue to cook the jam and try the test again after a few minutes.

Remove the jam from the heat and stir in the cinnamon. Ladle the jam into the clean, warm jars, leaving ¼ inch (6 mm) of headspace at the top. Bubble the jars and wipe the rims with a damp cloth. Place the lids on the jars and screw on the rings just until you feel resistance. Process the jars in a boiling water bath for 10 minutes. Allow to cool in the water for 5 minutes before removing. Store in a cool, dark place for up to 1 year.

PLUM LEKVAR (PLUM BUTTER)

Plum preserves and plum brandy are both very typical of central European, not just Ashkenazi, cuisine. Plum plants require a long period of winter chilling, making them suitable for the harsh climate of that part of the world. The season for plums was short, so thrifty housewives often dried the fruit, which they could use for compotes and cakes throughout the winter.

Plum butter was another popular way to preserve this abundant fruit. Fruit butters are so named not because they contain dairy, which would have prevented them from being eaten with a meat meal according to the kosher laws, but because they are as thick and spreadable as butter. Before the nineteenth century, when sugar was still a luxury item for Jews in eastern Europe and Russia, fruit butters, known as *fruit lekvar*, were extremely popular because they could be made with very little sugar, relying instead on the fiber of the fruit for their texture. Jewish immigrants were responsible for popularizing plum lekvar in America.

This spread has a rich, winey taste that makes it delicious on bread or spooned into yogurt. Plum butter is also an excellent filling for hamantaschen, the classic Purim dessert. I like to make several jars of plum butter in late summer or early fall, when plums are in season, and save at least one to fill my hamantaschen come March.

6 pounds (2.7 kg) Sterling,
    Stanley, or other European
    plums, pitted and roughly
    chopped
¾ cup (175 ml) water
2 to 2½ cups (400 to 500 g) sugar
Juice of 1 lemon

»» MAKES FIVE 8-OUNCE (235 ML) JARS «««

Place the plums in a large stockpot with the water. Bring to a boil, stirring occasionally. Reduce the heat to medium-low and cover. Simmer, stirring occasionally, until the fruit is softened and breaking down, about 30 to 40 minutes. Remove the pot from the heat and let it cool slightly.

Run the fruit and juices through a food mill using the finest screen to create a smooth pulp, straining out the skins and any tough fibers. If you don't have a food mill, purée the plums using an immersion blender and then strain through a fine-mesh sieve to remove the skins. Measure the plum pulp; you should have approximately 8 cups (1.8 kg).

Return the plum pulp to the stockpot and add 2 cups (400 g) of sugar. Stir to combine and bring the mixture to a boil over high heat. Once the liquid boils, reduce the heat to medium-low and let the mixture simmer until it is quite thick. This may take 2½ to 4 hours. It may bubble quite a bit; use a splatter screen on the pot as necessary. As it thickens, stir more frequently to prevent scorching.

The butter is done when it is much thicker and will mound on a spoon without giving off juices. It will have a silky texture and be a deep purple color.

When the butter is close to done, prepare a boiling water bath and heat five 8-ounce (235 ml) jars. Taste the plum butter; if it needs more sweetness, add up to ½ cup (100 g) sugar. Keep it on the heat for a few more minutes, stirring to dissolve the sugar. When it reaches the desired sweetness, remove it from the heat. Stir in the lemon juice.

Ladle the plum butter into the clean, warm jars, leaving ½ inch (1 cm) of headspace at the top. Bubble the jars and wipe the rims with a damp cloth. Place the lids on the jars and screw on the rings just until you feel resistance. Process the jars in a boiling water bath for 15 minutes. Allow to cool in the water for 5 minutes before removing. Store in a cool, dark place for up to 6 months.*

*Because fruit butters contain less sugar than jams, they have a shorter shelf life.

FRUITFUL FIG JAM

One of the first cultivated fruits, figs are as meaningful and symbolic as they are sweet and delicious. Jews consider figs to be particularly holy because they were one of the seven staple foods, known as the *Seven Species*, eaten by Jews in the land of Israel during Biblical times. Because they produce multiple crops every year, fig trees symbolize fruitfulness in Jewish literature. The medieval Jewish philosopher and scholar Maimonides considered figs, grapes, and almonds to be the best of fruits.

Native to the Middle East, figs are a common ingredient in Sephardic cooking in both fresh and dried form. As the largest crop of figs ripen in the fall, they are often served at Sephardic Rosh Hashanah celebrations. Every year, I feel a little giddy when I spy fresh figs in the grocery store because they are such a treat to preserve and their season in the United States is so brief. Because jam made from fresh figs is a classic Sephardic preserve, I have added some Sephardic flavors, orange and cinnamon, to this sunny, fresh-tasting spread. Try it as an accompaniment to cheese.

3 pounds (1.4 kg) whole figs, diced
½ cup (120 ml) water
3½ cups (700 g) sugar
⅓ cup (80 ml) lemon juice
Zest of 1 orange
¾ teaspoon cinnamon

Figs

"The fig tree has put forth its green figs, and the vines with their tiny grapes have given forth their fragrance; arise, my beloved, my fair one, and come away."
—Song of Songs 2:13

▶▶▶ MAKES SIX 8-OUNCE (235 ML) JARS ◀◀◀

Prepare a boiling water bath and heat six 8-ounce (235 ml) jars. Place a saucer in the freezer to chill.

Place the figs in a wide, deep saucepan and cover with the water.

Add the sugar and lemon juice and bring to a boil over medium-high heat, stirring to dissolve the sugar. Turn the heat down to medium and boil hard, stirring frequently to prevent scorching, until the jam thickens and fruit breaks down, about 10 to 15 minutes.

Remove the saucer from the freezer and place a dollop of jam on it. Return it to the freezer for 1 minute. Remove the saucer and push the dollop of jam with your finger. If it wrinkles, then the jam is set. If not, continue to cook the jam and try the test again after a few minutes.

Remove the jam from the heat and stir in the orange zest and cinnamon. Ladle the jam into the clean, warm jars, leaving ¼ inch (6 mm) of headspace at the top. Bubble the jars and wipe the rims with a damp cloth. Place the lids on the jars and screw on the rings just until you feel resistance.

Process the jars in a boiling water bath for 10 minutes. Allow to cool in the water for 5 minutes before removing. Store in a cool, dark place for up to 1 year.

GREENGAGE PLUM JAM

Tiny greengage plums, called *Reine Claude* in French, are prized throughout Europe for their luscious honey-like flavor, firm texture, and floral aroma. With skins containing a good amount of pectin, greengage plums were typically used by Eastern European Jews to make jam. Because the greengage has such a delicate flavor, I keep this jam very simple with just sugar, lemon juice, and a hint of vanilla. Sadly, during the cooking process, the greengages lose their beautiful color and the final product is somewhat murky. It still tastes heavenly.

It can be difficult to find greengage plums. Almost no European growers export these delicate fruits to the United States. Some American farmers have begun to cultivate their own trees, so, depending on where you live, most notably New York or California, you may have luck at your local farmers' market.

For most of us, however, the best bet for finding greengage plums is to look for those imported from New Zealand in late February and March. Although I seek out locally grown fruit whenever possible, greengages are so special that it is worth making an exception. Though greengages were a traditional Rosh Hashanah food for my European ancestors, for me, they may become a Purim treat.

2 quarts greengage plums (about 3 pounds, or 1.4 kg), halved and pitted
3 cups (600 g) sugar
Juice of 1 lemon
1 vanilla bean, cut in half and split lengthwise

▶▶▶ MAKES FIVE 8-OUNCE (235 ML) JARS ◀◀◀

Place the plums, sugar, lemon juice, and vanilla bean in a large Dutch oven and allow to sit for 1 hour. The sugar will pull the juice from the plums and create a syrupy mixture.

Prepare a boiling water bath and heat five 8-ounce (235 ml) jars. Place a saucer in the freezer to chill. Bring the plum mixture to a boil over medium-high heat, stirring to dissolve the sugar. Turn the heat down to medium and boil gently, adjusting the heat as necessary, until thickened and the jam reaches 220°F (104°C) on a candy thermometer, about 25 minutes.

Remove the saucer from the freezer and place a dollop of jam on it. Return it to the freezer for 1 minute. Remove the saucer and push the dollop of jam with your finger. If it wrinkles, then the jam is set. If not, continue to cook and try the test again after a few minutes.

Remove the vanilla bean. Ladle the jam into the clean, warm jars, leaving ¼ inch (6 mm) of headspace at the top. Bubble the jars and wipe the rims with a damp cloth. Place the lids on the jars and screw on the rings just until you feel resistance. Process the jars in a boiling water bath for 10 minutes. Allow to cool in the water for 5 minutes before removing. Store in a cool, dark place for up to 1 year.

ABRAHAM'S GREENGAGE CHUTNEY

Sephardic Jews call sour plums *avramila* or Abraham's fruit because of the legend that Abraham sat under a plum tree—presumably to recover—after being circumcised. Among Greek Jews, Fish with Abraham's Fruit, or fish with a spiced greengage plum sauce, is a traditional Rosh Hashanah dish. It is not unusual to see greengages used in savory dishes in other parts of the world as well: the English pair greengage chutney with oily fish, such as mackerel.

Because not many Americans care for mackerel, I suggest pairing this greengage chutney with cheese, anything from a nutty Gruyère to a creamy Brie.

6 cups (990 g) sliced and pitted greengage plums
1½ cups (340 g) brown sugar
1 cup (235 ml) apple cider vinegar
¾ cup (110 g) golden raisins
½ cup (80 g) diced yellow onion
2 teaspoons yellow mustard seeds
¾ teaspoon ground ginger
¾ teaspoon ground cloves
½ teaspoon pickling salt
¼ teaspoon ground allspice

▶▶▶ MAKES 2 PINTS (950 ML) ◀◀◀

Prepare a boiling water bath and heat 2 pint (475 ml) jars.

Combine all of the ingredients in a large, wide Dutch oven and stir to combine. Bring to a boil over high heat, stirring to dissolve the sugar. Turn the heat down to medium and simmer the chutney until it is thick enough to mound up on a spoon, about 30 minutes. You may need to turn the heat down to medium-low or even low to keep the chutney at a simmer and prevent scorching.

Ladle the chutney into the jars, leaving ½ inch (1 cm) of headspace. Bubble the jars and wipe the rims with a damp cloth. Place the lids on the jars and screw on the rings just until you feel resistance. Process the jars in a boiling water bath for 15 minutes. Allow to cool in the water for 5 minutes before removing. Allow to cure for 2 to 3 weeks before opening for the best results. Store in a cool, dark place for up to 1 year.

CRANBERRY APPLESAUCE

Applesauce is one of the best-known and best-loved Jewish preserves because it is one of the two traditional toppings for potato pancakes or *latkes*. (The other being sour cream. The arguments over which topping is better can get rather heated.) *Latkes* are a Jewish deli staple, but are perhaps best known as the traditional dish for the festival of Hanukkah, at least among Ashkenazi Jews.

In Europe, Ashkenazi Jews often made a version of applesauce that included foraged berries, such as raspberries or blackberries. I have updated that tradition by adding cranberries, that quint-essential North American berry, to my applesauce. The cranberries add tartness and a beautiful rosy color. Make this crimson-hued applesauce in October when whole cranberries and heirloom varieties of apples are readily available at farmers' markets and put up several jars to accompany your Hanukkah latkes in December. You may even convert some sour cream partisans to your side.

4 pounds (1.8 kg) apples,
    preferably a mixture of sweet
    and tart varieties
2 cups (200 g) whole cranberries
    (fresh or frozen)
1 cup (120 ml) water
¼ cup (60 ml) lemon juice
1¼ cups (250 g) sugar
½ teaspoon cinnamon
¼ teaspoon ground cloves

▶▶▶ MAKES 3 TO 4 PINTS (1.4 TO 1.9 L) ◀◀◀

Peel, core, and roughly chop the apples. Combine the apples, cranberries, water, and lemon juice in a large saucepan. Bring the liquid to a boil, turn down the heat to low, and simmer, covered, stirring occasionally.

Meanwhile, prepare a boiling water bath and heat 4 pint (475 ml) jars.

When the apples are tender, about 30 to 45 minutes depending on the varieties you use, remove from the heat. Mash the apples with a potato masher. For a smoother texture, purée with an immersion blender but leave some chunkiness. Add the sugar and spices and return the mixture to a simmer, stirring to dissolve the sugar and distribute the spices.

Ladle the sauce into the clean, warm jars, leaving ¾ inch (2 cm) of headspace. Bubble the jars well because the sauce is so thick and wipe the rims with a damp cloth. Place the lids on the jars and screw on the rings just until you feel resistance. Process the jars in a boiling water bath for 15 minutes. Allow to cool in the water for 5 minutes before removing. Store in a cool, dark place for up to 1 year.

CHAROSET CONSERVE

One of the most important symbolic foods for Passover is *charoset*, a fruit mixture that is eaten twice during the Seder ritual. Charoset represents the mortar that the Jewish slaves used to build the Pharaoh's pyramids. While charoset for Passover is common across all Jewish people, the form it takes—that is, what ingredients it is based on—truly reflects regional differences. Fresh fruit, dried fruit, honey, spices, wine, and nuts are all common charoset ingredients. However your charoset is made, it should be sweet and delicious.

For the Ashkenazi Jews, apples became the basis for traditional charoset recipes, along with honey, wine, cinnamon, and nuts, because they could be kept in cold storage from the fall until Passover, which takes place before most fruits have come into season. This conserve recipe is inspired by the flavors of traditional Ashkenazi charoset. I often make it in the fall when apples are in season, and I give it as a holiday gift. It is always very well received.

8 cups (1 kg) peeled and chopped apples

1 cup (235 ml) grape juice or sweet wine such as Manischewitz

½ cup (120 ml) apple juice or cider

1 cup (340 g) honey

½ cup (100 g) sugar

Juice of 2 lemons

1 teaspoon cinnamon

½ teaspoon ground cloves

½ cup (60 g) chopped black walnuts, lightly toasted

2 tablespoons (28 ml) apple brandy or Calvados (optional)

>>> MAKES FIVE 8-OUNCE (235 ML) JARS <<<

Combine the apples, grape juice, and apple juice in a large, deep saucepan. Bring to a boil. Turn down the heat, cover, and simmer until the apples are tender, about 10 minutes.

While the apples are simmering, prepare a boiling water bath and heat five 8-ounce (235 ml) jars.

Mash the apples by hand using a potato masher to achieve a chunky consistency. Add the honey, sugar, and lemon juice to the apple mixture and bring to a boil over medium heat, stirring to dissolve the sugar. Continue to boil the mixture gently, stirring frequently to prevent scorching. The conserve will spit, so use caution.

Boil until the mixture reaches 220°F (104°C) and is thick enough to mound up on a spoon without liquid pooling around the edges, about 15 minutes. Remove the conserve from the heat and stir in the spices and walnuts. Add the apple brandy (if using).

Ladle the conserve into the clean, warm jars, leaving ¼ inch (6 mm) of headspace at the top. Bubble the jars and wipe the rims with a damp cloth. Place the lids on the jars and screw on the rings just until you feel resistance. Process the jars in a boiling water bath for 10 minutes. Allow to cool in the water for 5 minutes before removing. Store in a cool, dark place for up to 1 year.

APPLE BUTTER

Apples were an important fruit for Ashkenazi Jews because they grew abundantly in northern and central Europe and Russia and could be kept in cold storage all winter. Apples appear in Ashkenazi holiday foods from Rosh Hashanah to Passover. But did you know that in Jewish tradition the apple was not the forbidden fruit that Eve ate in the Garden of Eden? Some scholars theorize that notorious fruit was, in fact, an apricot.

For apple butter, use a soft apple that will cook down fast, such as Braeburn, Cortland, Fuji, McIntosh, or Ida Red. You can even use a variety of apples for the best flavor. Straining the apples through a sieve or food mill is somewhat tedious but the result, a silky-smooth butter, is worth it.

6 pounds (2.7 kg) apples, peeled, cored, and coarsely chopped
2 cups (475 ml) apple cider
1½ cups (300 g) sugar
½ cup (115 g) brown sugar
1 teaspoon ground cinnamon
¼ teaspoon ground allspice

▶▶▶ MAKES SIX TO SEVEN 8-OUNCE (235 ML) JARS ◀◀◀

Place the apples in a large stockpot or Dutch oven and add the apple cider. Bring to a boil, stirring occasionally. Reduce the heat to medium-low and cover. Let simmer, stirring occasionally, until the fruit is breaking down, about 40 minutes.

Remove the pot from the heat. Working in batches, push the apples and accumulated juices through a sieve into a large bowl, straining out any fibers or seed particles to create a smooth pulp. Alternatively, you can use a food mill set on the finest screen. Measure the apple pulp. You should have about 8 cups (2 L).

Return the apple mixture to the stockpot and add the sugars. Stir to combine and bring to a boil over high heat. Reduce the heat to medium-low and let the mixture simmer until it is reduced by about half and quite thick, about 1½ to 2 hours. The apple butter will spit quite a bit; use a splatter screen on the pot as necessary.

Toward the end of the cooking, prepare a boiling water bath and heat seven 8-ounce (235 ml) jars. As the butter thickens, stir more frequently to prevent scorching. When the butter mounds on a spoon without giving off liquid, it is done. Remove from the heat, add the spices, and stir well to evenly disperse them.

Ladle the butter into the jars, leaving ½ inch (1 cm) of headspace. Bubble the jars and wipe the rims. Place the lids on the jars and screw on the rings just until you feel resistance. Process the jars in a boiling water bath for 15 minutes. Allow to cool in the water for 5 minutes before removing. Store in a cool, dark place for up to 6 months.*

Because fruit butters contain less sugar than jams, they have a shorter shelf life.

APPLE MINT JELLY

Apple mint jelly, which most people think of as something to eat with lamb, may seem more British than anything else. But some scholars have speculated that combining lamb and mint is the legacy of the Passover tradition of eating lamb with bitter herbs. Both apples and mint are among the foods mentioned in the Talmud and were part of the diet of Jews since Biblical times. For the Ashkenazi Jews of Poland and Russia, fruits, such as apples, cherries, and plums, were more abundant than vegetables and sometimes were used as an accompaniment to meat.

As with all jellies, this recipe is a bit labor-intensive because you first have to strain the juice from the fruit and then make the jelly. The result, however, is a pale gold, translucent jelly with a sweet apple flavor and just a hint of mint. Apple mint jelly is a delightful accompaniment to roast lamb and also duck. Use it to glaze pastries or just enjoy it on toast. Because of its stunning color, this jelly makes an impressive gift.

5 pounds (2.3 kg) apples,
*   quartered*
5 cups (1.2 L) water
1 cup (35 g) fresh mint leaves,
*   tightly packed*
3 to 4 cups (600 to 800 g) sugar
2 tablespoons (28 ml) lemon juice

Mint

There are many varieties of mint grown in home gardens. Each will offer a slightly different flavor to this jelly, allowing you to develop your own "signature" flavor. Avoid chocolate mint, which does not mix well with apple.

>>> MAKES FOUR TO FIVE 8-OUNCE (235 ML) JARS <<<

Begin by extracting the juice from the apples. To do this, place the apple quarters and water in a large saucepan and bring to a boil. Reduce the heat and boil gently, with the pot partially covered, until the apples are tender enough to crush with a wooden spoon, about 20 to 30 minutes. Do not overcook because that will affect how the jelly sets.

Line a colander with several layers of damp cheesecloth and place it over a tall stockpot. Ladle the apple mixture into the colander and allow the juice to drain into the pot undisturbed for at least 2 hours. Do not press on the apples because that will result in a cloudy jelly.

After the apples have stopped draining, measure the juice. You could end up with anywhere from 4 to 6 cups (940 ml to 1.4 L) of juice depending on the variety of apples you used and how long you allowed the juice to drain. Make a note of the amount of juice because it will determine how much sugar to use. Pour the juice into a storage container. Discard the remaining apple pulp.

Crush the mint leaves gently with your fingers to release the oils and add to the apple juice. Cover this mixture and refrigerate for at least 8 hours and up to 2 days.

To make the jelly, prepare a boiling water bath and heat five 8-ounce (235 ml) jars. Place a saucer in the freezer to chill.

Pour the apple juice into a large deep saucepan, straining out the mint leaves. Press on the mint leaves to extract as much juice as possible. If you have 4 cups (950 ml) of apple juice, add 3 cups (600 g) of

sugar; for 5 cups (1.2 L) of juice, add 3½ cups sugar (700 g); and for 6 cups (1.4 L) of juice, add 4 cups (800 g) of sugar.

Combine the apple juice, sugar, and lemon juice in a large, deep saucepan. The jelly will bubble up substantially, so select a large pot. Bring the mixture to a boil over high heat, stirring to dissolve the sugar. Reduce the heat to medium-high and boil the mixture hard, stirring frequently until it begins to gel, about 20 minutes.

Remove the saucer from the freezer and place a dollop of jelly on it. Return it to the freezer for 1 minute. Remove the saucer and push the dollop of jelly with your finger. If it wrinkles, then the jelly is set. If not, continue to cook and try the test again after a few minutes. Skim off any foam that has accumulated.

Ladle the jelly into the jars, leaving ¼ inch (6 mm) of headspace. Bubble the jars and wipe the rims with a damp cloth. Place the lids on the jars and screw on the rings just until you feel resistance. Process the jars in a boiling water bath for 10 minutes. Allow to cool in the water for 5 minutes before removing. Store in a cool, dark place for up to 1 year.

APPLE, HONEY, AND ROSE WATER JAM

This special preserve combines traditional foods and flavors for Rosh Hashanah in both Ashkenazi and Sephardic cuisine. Apples being a fall crop are plentiful at Rosh Hashanah. Beginning Rosh Hashanah dinner by dipping apples into honey, to symbolize the hope for a sweet new year, is nearly universal among Eastern European Jews. The Sephardim often end their new year's celebrations with sweet jams and preserves made from quince, figs, dates, and apples.

Rose water, which is made by distilling fresh rose petals in water, is featured in many Sephardic desserts and pastries. It can be purchased at Middle Eastern grocers and specialty food stores. Rose water has a very strong flavor and should be used sparingly or it can overwhelm your palate. Here, it adds a haunting floral note to this unusual, pale yellow jam.

3 pounds (1.4 kg) apples, peeled, cored, and cut into ½-inch (1 cm) dice (approximately 6 to 7 cups [1 kg] prepped)
½ cup (120 ml) water
2 tablespoons (28 ml) lemon juice
1½ cups (300 g) sugar
1 cup (340 g) honey
1 teaspoon rose water

»» MAKES FOUR 8-OUNCE (235 ML) JARS ««

Prepare a boiling water bath and heat four 8-ounce (235 ml) jars. Place a saucer in the freezer to chill.

Place the apples, water, and lemon juice in a wide, deep saucepan. Bring to a boil over high heat, stir, and cover the pot. Lower the heat to medium and cook until the apples are soft, about 10 minutes, stirring once or twice to prevent sticking or burning. Mash the apples coarsely with a fork or potato masher.

Add the sugar and honey to the pot, stirring to dissolve. Return to a boil over medium-high heat.

Continue to cook, stirring frequently, until the mixture is thick and mounds up on a spoon, about 10 to 15 minutes. It will splatter, so use caution. Remove the saucer from the freezer and place a dollop of jam on it. Return to the freezer for 1 minute. Remove it and push the jam with your fingers. If it wrinkles, the jam is set. If not, continue to cook and try the test again after a few minutes.

Remove the jam from the heat and stir in the rose water. Ladle the jam into the clean, warm jars, leaving ¼ inch (6 mm) of headspace at the top. Bubble the jars and wipe the rims with a damp cloth. Place the lids on the jars and screw on the rings just until you feel resistance. Process the jars in a boiling water bath for 10 minutes. Allow to cool in the water for 5 minutes before removing. Store in a cool, dark place for up to 1 year.

DULCE DE MANZANA (APPLE PASTE)

Turkish Jews, whose origins trace back to the Jews' expulsion from Spain in 1492, express their hopes for a sweet new year by partaking in *dulce de manzana*, a firm, sweet apple paste. In the Sephardic world, dulce de manzana is often infused with vanilla or with rose water. I flavor my version of dulce de manzana with spices that Americans associate with apples, such as cinnamon and nutmeg.

Cut into squares and tossed with sugar, these apple jellies are similar to *pâté de fruit*. They make an elegant sweet bite to serve after a meal. Children love them as a homemade version of packaged fruit snacks. You can also cut the paste into larger blocks and serve them with a cheese plate as one would with quince paste.

3 pounds (1.4 kg) apples, a mix of hard and soft varieties such as Granny Smith and McIntosh

1 cup (235 ml) water

1 cup (200 g) sugar

¼ cup (60 g) brown sugar

½ teaspoon ground cinnamon

⅛ teaspoon ground nutmeg

Juice of 1 lemon

Additional sugar, for coating the candies

▶▶▶ MAKES 100 SQUARES ◀◀◀

Quarter the apples, cutting off the stem and blossom, but do not core or peel. The natural pectins in those parts will help the candies to set.

Combine the apples and water in a low, wide pan with a lid. Bring to a boil over high heat and then reduce the heat to medium-low, cover, and simmer until very soft, about 20 minutes. Remove from the heat, uncover, and allow to cool slightly to make them easier to work with. Process the apples in batches using a food mill on the finest screen. Alternatively, press the apples through a sieve to catch all the skins, seeds, and cores.

Return the apple pulp to the pan, and add the remaining ingredients. Stir well to combine.

Cook over low heat, stirring frequently, until the mixture becomes a thick paste. Use a splatter screen as necessary. The length of cooking time will vary depending on the natural moisture of your apples, but it will be at least an hour. A spoon drawn through the mixture should leave a clear channel that remains for a few seconds.

To test the doneness, chill a small amount on a plate in the freezer. It should appear and feel jellied. Lightly coat a 9 x 9-inch (23 x 23 cm) baking dish with cooking spray or another neutral oil. Do not use a smaller pan or the mixture will be too thick and may not set. If you must use a smaller pan, divide the mixture among two pans.

Spread evenly in the pan and set aside to allow it to set up, at least 8 hours or overnight. When set, invert the paste onto a lined baking sheet to expose the bottom of the paste. Allow this to dry for another 8 to 12 hours. The paste can be stored, wrapped in plastic, in the refrigerator and will keep for months.

MEMBRILLO (QUINCE PASTE FOR ROSH HASHANAH)

Quince's high pectin content makes it amenable to being turned into pastes and gels. You may know quince paste as *membrillo* and associate it with Spanish cuisine, but it is a classic Sephardic sweet as well. Indeed, quince paste is a traditional Rosh Hashanah and Succot food.

The tradition of candied fruits and jellied candies developed early in Sephardic cuisine because sugar was readily accessible as early as the Middle Ages when it was cultivated in North Africa and spread throughout the region by the Arabs. Still, sugar remained too expensive for most Ashkenazi Jews to use in large quantities until the nineteenth century.

Serve quince paste with cheese. It pairs particularly well with hard cheeses, such as Manchego.

2½ pounds (1.2 kg) quince (approximately 5 pieces of fruit)
¼ cup (60 ml) water or apple juice
3 cups (600 g) sugar
Juice of 1 lemon

»»» MAKES 16 SQUARES «««

Preheat the oven to 350°F (180°C, or gas mark 4).

Wash any fuzz off the exterior of the quince. Place the quince in a baking dish and cover with foil. Bake until it is quite soft, about 90 minutes to 2 hours. Remove from the heat and allow to cool. Slip the skins off and cut the flesh from the core. Discard the skins and cores.

Place the quince flesh in the food processor with the water or apple juice and purée until smooth. Measure the remaining purée. You should have about 3 cups (700 ml). Pour the purée into a large, deep saucepan. Add an equal amount of sugar by volume. So for 3 cups of purée, add 3 cups (600 g) of sugar.

Add the lemon juice and bring the mixture to a boil, stirring to dissolve the sugar. Turn down the heat to medium-low and simmer the quince, uncovered, until it is so thick that the spoon leaves a clear track when you stir, about 20 to 25 minutes. Stir frequently to prevent scorching, especially as the paste thickens. The quince purée will spit; use caution.

Spray an 8 x 8-inch (20 x 20 cm) or 9 x 9-inch (23 x 23 cm) square baking pan with nonstick cooking spray and pour in the quince. Spread in an even layer. Place the pan in the refrigerator to chill for several hours. When the top is firm and no longer tacky, cut the quince paste into 16 squares. Wrap each square in parchment paper or plastic wrap and tie with baker's twine for a charming presentation. Quince paste will keep in refrigerator for months.

ROSY QUINCE JELLY

Quince is notoriously astringent and cannot be eaten raw. It becomes soft and palatable when baked or poached and sweetened with sugar or honey. Because of its high pectin content, quince was one of the first fruits used to make jam and jelly. Indeed, for centuries, quince was the most common kind of fruit preserve. The word marmalade, which today we associate with citrus fruit, actually derives from the Portuguese word for quince, *marmelo*.

Sephardis have multiple ways of cooking and preserving this cherished fruit. Making jelly from quince juice is a convenient way to cook with this somewhat difficult fruit because there is no need to peel or chop it. And with its rosy pink color and floral aroma, quince jelly is an exceptionally lovely preserve. Spread it on toast, spoon it into yogurt, or pair some with a cheese plate. Quince jelly also makes a stunning gift.

Once you have cooked with quince, you may find yourself as entranced as those in the Middle East who cherish this ancient crop. Use it in baked goods or for preserving or in meat stews as the Sephardim do.

3 pounds (1.4 kg) quince (about six)

6 cups (1. 4 L) water

3 cups (600 g) sugar (approximately)

2 tablespoons (28 ml) lemon juice

1 vanilla bean

6 whole cloves

▶▶▶ MAKES THREE 8-OUNCE (235 ML) JARS ◀◀◀

Wash the quince well and cut into quarters, trimming off the blossom end. Use a sharp knife and be cautious when cutting because quince are very hard.

Add the quince to a large, deep saucepan and cover with water. Bring the mixture to a boil and then turn down the heat and simmer, covered, for 1 to 1½ hours until the fruit is tender.

Line a fine-mesh sieve with a layer of damp cheesecloth and set it over a deep bowl. Carefully ladle the juice and fruit from the saucepan into the sieve. Allow the juice to drip for several hours or even overnight. Do not press on the fruit because that can make the jelly cloudy.

Prepare a boiling water bath and heat three 8-ounce (235 ml) jars. Place a saucer in the freezer to chill.

Measure the juice. You should have 3 to 4 cups (700 to 950 ml). For each cup (235 ml) of juice, you want to use slightly less than 1 cup (200 g) of sugar. So for 3 cups (700 ml) of juice, use 2½ cups (500 g) of sugar. For 4 cups (950 ml) of juice, use 3 cups (600 g) of sugar.

Combine the juice, sugar, lemon juice, and vanilla bean in a large, deep saucepan. Tie the cloves in a small spice bag and add them to the pot. Bring the mixture to a boil, stirring to dissolve the sugar. Boil until the mixture reaches 220°F (104°C), about 10 to 15 minutes.

Remove the saucer from the freezer and place a dollop of jelly on it. Return it to the freezer for 1 minute. Remove the saucer and push the

Finding Quince

Quince have been cultivated since ancient times, long before the ubiquitous apple. For this reason, some scholars believe that the quince, not the apple, is the proper translation for the Hebrew word *tapuach*, a fruit mentioned in the Biblical Song of Songs. The Talmud specifically mentions the quince as well, and it prescribes a blessing to be said for its distinctive aroma. That aroma makes quince a delight to cook with and eat.

Quince are in season in the Western Hemisphere in the fall. Look for quince at your farmers' market in September or October. If you do not see them, ask the vendors. Some growers raise quince, but do not typically bring them to markets because of low demand. The vendor who brings me quince every fall charges me the same price for them as he does for apples, which is a very good deal. You can also find quince in better grocery stores in the fall, but they will likely be more expensive. I have also seen quince in the grocery store in early spring when they are imported from South America.

dollop of jelly with your finger. If it wrinkles, then the jelly is set. If not, continue to cook and try the test again after a few minutes. The jelly in the pot may appear to be somewhat liquid even when it is done; it will gel more upon cooling. Remove from the heat and allow the boiling to subside. Discard the vanilla bean and cloves. Skim off any foam that has accumulated.

Ladle the jelly into the jars, leaving ¼ inch (6 mm) of headspace at the top. Bubble the jars and wipe the rims with a damp cloth. If there is any foam on the top of the jars, skim that off as well. You want a translucent final product. Place the lids on the jars and screw on the rings just until you feel resistance. Process the jars in a boiling water bath for 10 minutes. Allow to cool in the water for 5 minutes before removing. Store in a cool, dark place for up to 1 year.

GOLDEN PUMPKIN BUTTER FOR ROSH HASHANAH

Sephardic Jews have a particular tradition of serving foods with symbolic meanings during Rosh Hashanah. These symbolic meanings often derive from puns on the name of the food. For example, the word for squash or pumpkin in Hebrew is *qara*, which sounds like the Hebrew verbs for "to rip or tear up" and "to read or call out." Thus, it is traditional to eat pumpkins or squash at Rosh Hashanah. Before doing so, it is customary to recite a special prayer that any harsh decrees that may have been issued be "torn up" and that the speaker's merits be "read out" before the Creator.

Pumpkin butter is a quick and easy project, and the result tastes like fall in a jar. Spread it on whole-wheat toast or spoon some into vanilla yogurt. You will notice that I do not include instructions for processing this butter in a boiling water bath. It is not safe to water-bath can pumpkin in any form because of the vegetable's density. If 3 cups (700 ml) is too much for your family, you can freeze some. Or consider packaging the extra in a nice jar and bringing it as a gift to your hosts when you are invited to Rosh Hashanah dinner.

1 small pie pumpkin

1 to 2 cups (200 to 400 g) sugar

2 tablespoons (28 ml) lemon juice

½ teaspoon cinnamon

¼ teaspoon ground ginger

⅛ teaspoon nutmeg

Pinch of white pepper

»» MAKES 3 CUPS (700 ML) ««

Preheat the oven to 400°F (200°C, or gas mark 6).

Remove the stem from the pumpkin, carefully cut it in half, and scrape out the seeds. Fit it into a baking dish, cut sides down, filled with ½ inch (1 cm) of water. Cover tightly with foil and bake until very soft, about 45 minutes.

When the pumpkin halves are cool enough to handle, scrape out the flesh and mash with a fork or for a smoother texture, purée in a food processor. Measure the mashed or puréed pumpkin.

Measure out half that amount of sugar. For example, if you have 2½ cups (613 g) of pumpkin purée, use 1¼ cups (250 g) of sugar.

Place the sugar and pumpkin in a large, deep saucepan. Stir in the lemon juice. Over medium heat, bring the mixture to a slow and careful boil, stirring to dissolve the sugar. The mixture will bubble, so exercise caution and use a splatter screen if necessary. Let the mixture cook for 10 to 15 minutes, stirring frequently to prevent scorching, until thick and spreadable.

Remove from the heat, stir in the spices, and mix well to incorporate. Store in the refrigerator or freeze.

SUGAR PEARS IN VANILLA SYRUP

Pears are mentioned in the Talmud and have been cultivated by humans since antiquity. The ancient Romans grew dozens of varieties, which they ate both raw and cooked. Along with apple, plums, and cherries, pears were one of the fruits that grew abundantly in the forests of eastern Europe, Poland, and Russia. Pears were a common ingredient in fruit compote, which was a typical way to end a weekday meal. Whole poached pears were considered an elegant dessert suitable for a holiday meal, such as Passover Seder.

For these whole pears in vanilla syrup, I use diminutive Seckel pears that are so sweet they are called "sugar pears." They make for a beautiful presentation. For a light dessert, plate a few of these pears with a dollop of crème fraîche and a drizzle of the vanilla syrup.

3½ cups (700 g) sugar

7 cups (1.6 L) water

5 pounds (2.3 kg) Seckel pears, slightly firm

1 lemon, halved

2 tablespoons (30 g) vanilla bean paste, or 2 whole vanilla beans, split and seeds scraped

»» MAKES 4 QUARTS (3.8 L) ««

Prepare a boiling water bath and heat 4 quart (950 ml) jars.

In a large stockpot, combine the sugar and water. Bring to a boil, stirring to dissolve the sugar.

While the syrup is coming to a boil, prepare the pears. To prevent the pears from browning, fill a large bowl with cold water, squeeze the juice from the lemons into the bowl, and then add the lemon halves. Peel the pears, carefully carving out the blossom end and cut off the stem. Add each pear to the lemon water as you finish preparing it. Do not let the pears sit in the water for more than 20 minutes or they will get soggy.

When the sugar syrup comes to a boil, reduce the heat. Add the vanilla bean paste. If using whole beans, add the seeds and pods at this time. Stir well to combine and keep at very low heat as you finish preparing the pears.

Carefully add the peeled pears to the vanilla syrup, one layer at a time. Raise the heat to medium and cook until warmed through, about 5 minutes. Gently press on the pears or rotate them to ensure that each one has been thoroughly bathed in syrup.

To fill the clean jars, turn one on its side and gently add one pear at a time. About five pears will fit in each jar. If using whole vanilla beans, add half a pod to each jar.

Ladle the syrup over the pears in the jars, leaving 1 inch (2.5 cm) of headspace. Bubble the jars, adding more syrup if necessary, and wipe the rims with a damp cloth. Place the lids on the jars and screw on the rings just until you feel resistance. Process the jars in a boiling water bath for 25 minutes. Allow to cool in the water for 5 minutes before removing. Store in a cool, dark place for up to 1 year.

GALICIAN PEAR BUTTER

The Jews of Galicia and southern Russia made a traditional *tzimmes* from apples, pears, figs, and dried plums known as *floymn tzimes*. Indeed, pears are often combined with apples in Ashkenazi cuisine whether in tzimmes, charoset, or preserves. I find, however, that apples overwhelm the delicate flavor of the pear. This smooth butter allows the pear to take center stage.

5 pounds (2.3 kg) pears, Bartlett preferred, peeled, cored, and coarsely chopped
1 cup (235 ml) water
1 cup (200 g) sugar
Juice of ½ of a lemon
¾ teaspoon ground ginger

▶▶▶ MAKES FOUR 8-OUNCE (235 ML) JARS ◀◀◀

Place the pears in a large stockpot and add the water. Bring to a boil, stirring occasionally. The boil may be hard to see because of the volume of fruit. Listen for the sound of large bubbles. Reduce the heat to medium-low and cover. Simmer, stirring occasionally, until the fruit is very soft and breaking down, about 30 to 40 minutes. Remove the pot from the heat and let it cool slightly.

Purée the fruit using an immersion blender or in batches in a food processor. Return the pear mixture to the stockpot and add the sugar. Stir to combine and bring it to a boil over high heat.

Reduce the heat to medium-low and let the mixture simmer until it is reduced by half and is quite thick, about 2 hours. It may bubble quite a bit; use a splatter screen on the pot as necessary. As it thickens, stir more frequently to prevent scorching.

Toward the end of the cooking, prepare a boiling water bath and heat four 8-ounce (235 ml) jars.

When the pear butter will mound on a spoon without giving off liquid, it is done. Remove from the heat, add the lemon juice and ginger, and stir well to combine.

Ladle the pear butter into the clean, warm jars, leaving ½ inch (1 cm) of headspace. Bubble the jars and wipe the rims with a damp cloth. Place the lids on the jars and screw on the rings just until you feel resistance. Process the jars in a boiling water bath for 15 minutes. Allow to cool in the water for 5 minutes before removing. Store in a cool, dark place for up to 6 months.*

*Because fruit butters contain less sugar than jams, they have a shorter shelf life.

POMEGRANATE JELLY

Mentioned in both the Bible and the Song of Songs, pomegranates play a significant role in Jewish literature and folklore. For centuries, pomegranate symbols adorned coins, priestly garb, and even Torah scrolls. Legend has it that a pomegranate contains 613 seeds, the same number as the number of commandments in the Torah.

Pomegranates ripen in fall, so for Sephardic Jews, they were traditional fare for Rosh Hashanah and Succot. Indeed, for Sephardim, the new year meal typically ended with fresh dates, figs, and pomegranates. Sephardic cooks also crushed the pomegranate seeds for juice which they then cooked down into a syrup and used to add tartness to their dishes.

If you like pomegranates, you will love the concentrated, tart flavor of this jelly. Pomegranates are low in pectin, so this preserve is not as firm as apple or quince jelly. Indeed, it is more the texture of a very thick syrup than a firm jelly. Pour a little into your yogurt, add some to cocktails, or use it in cooking and baking as one would do with pomegranate molasses. Add some to a favorite salad dressing or drizzle on fruit or even vegetables such as the roasted carrots at left.

4 cups (950 ml) pomegranate juice

3 cups (600 g) sugar

3 tablespoons (45 ml) lemon juice

▶▶▶ MAKES THREE 8-OUNCE (235 ML) JARS ◀◀◀

Prepare a boiling water bath and heat three 8-ounce (235 ml) jars. Place a saucer in the freezer to chill.

Combine the pomegranate juice, sugar, and lemon juice in a large saucepan. Bring the mixture to a boil, stirring to dissolve the sugar. Continue to boil until the mixture reaches 220°F (104°C) on a candy thermometer. Cook until the mixture has thickened and reduced by a third, about 20 minutes of total cooking time. The liquid should be thicker and slower to drip than maple syrup.

Remove the saucer from the freezer and place a dollop of jelly on it. Return it to the freezer for 1 minute. Remove the saucer and push the dollop of jelly with your finger. If it wrinkles, then the jelly is set. If not, continue to cook and try the test again after a few minutes.

Ladle the jelly into the clean, warm jars, leaving ¼ inch (6 mm) of headspace at the top. Bubble the jars and wipe the rims with a damp cloth. Place the lids on the jars and screw on the rings just until you feel resistance. Process the jars in a boiling water bath for 10 minutes. Allow to cool in the water for 5 minutes before removing. Store in a cool, dark place for up to 1 year.

SPICED PRUNE JAM

Dried plums, or prunes, were very important to Jews from the shtetls of Poland and Russia and thus appear often in traditional Ashkenazi cuisine. Plums grew abundantly on the outskirts of the villages in these countries, but the season for fresh plums was short. So women gathered the fruit not to eat fresh so much as to preserve for the winter in the form of plum butter or *lekvar*, dried prunes, and even fermented plum liquor.

Prunes appear in sweet Ashkenazi dishes, such as fruit compote and tzimmes, and they are found in savory ones, such as cholent. They have a reputation for being stodgy and eaten more for their dietary fiber than their taste. If you are a prune hater, or know one, this spiced prune jam will change your mind. Sure, it's thick and sweet, but with a lot of zesty, spicy flavor. This is a fun preserving project for the winter months.

8 ounces (225 g) pitted prunes, finely diced (about 1½ cups [263 g] diced prunes)

3 ounces (85 g) dried cherries, finely diced (about ½ cup [80g] diced dried cherries)

1 large apple, peeled, cored, and grated

1½ cups (300 g) sugar

1½ cups (355 ml) apple cider, apple juice, water, or a combination

Juice of 1 lemon

1 teaspoon ground ginger

½ teaspoon cinnamon

¼ teaspoon ground cloves

▶▶▶ MAKES FOUR 8-OUNCE (235 ML) JARS ◀◀◀

Prepare a boiling water bath and heat four 8-ounce (235 ml) jars.

Combine all of the ingredients in a large saucepan or Dutch oven. Bring to a boil over high heat, stirring to dissolve the sugar. Once the mixture boils, cover the pot, reduce the heat to medium-low, and cook for 20 minutes, stirring occasionally.

After 20 minutes, check the jam. The dried fruit should be very soft, the apples cooked down, and the liquid reduced to a thick syrup. If not, continue to cook for a few additional minutes.

Ladle the jam into the clean, warm jars, leaving ¼ inch (6 mm) of headspace at the top. Bubble the jars and wipe the rims with a damp cloth. Place the lids on the jars and screw on the rings just until you feel resistance. Process the jars in a boiling water bath for 10 minutes. Allow to cool in the water for 5 minutes before removing. Store in a cool, dark place for up to 1 year.

Using Dried Fruits

When making jam with dried fruit, chop the fruit into small dice (about ¼-inch [6 mm] pieces) because it will plump considerably when reconstituted with the cooking liquid. To prevent the fruit from making your knife sticky, carefully wipe the blade with a few drops of oil.

HALEK (DATE JAM)

Dates are an ancient food that have become trendy again as a natural alternative to refined sugars. Because they could be dried or cooked down to a thick, long-lasting syrup, dates were one of the first preserved foods and thus important to the diet of Biblical people. In fact, many scholars believe that the word "honey" in the phrase "the land of milk and honey" refers not to honey made by bees, but rather date syrup. The date palm tree also plays a prominent role in Jewish folklore and history, especially in the celebration of the festival of Succot.

Unlike date syrup, which is very labor-intensive to make, this date jam comes together quite quickly and the flavor is bright and sunny. Dates are low in acid and therefore are not safe to can in a boiling water bath except in combination with higher-acid fruits or with other acidic ingredients, such as vinegar, in the case of date chutney. Thus, this is a refrigerator jam. It will last for several weeks. Try it as a filling for cakes and bar cookies or as sweetener in smoothies and baked goods. Or, use it as a basis for a Sephardic-style charoset (see below).

2 pounds (910 g) Medjool dates
¼ cup (60 ml) lemon juice
½ teaspoon cinnamon
2 cups (495 ml) water
Zest of 1 orange

»» MAKES 2 PINTS (950 ML) ««

Pit and chop the dates. In a large saucepan, combine the dates, lemon juice, cinnamon, and water. Bring to a boil. Reduce the heat and simmer until thickened and the dates have broken down, about 10 minutes. Remove from the heat and add the orange zest.

You can leave the date jam as is or if you prefer a smoother texture, purée it using an immersion blender or food processor for 20 to 30 seconds. Ladle the jam into two clean and sterilized (page 26) pint (475 ml) jars. Store in the refrigerator.

How to Make Sephardic Date Charoset

Dates are the basis for many of the charoset recipes from the Sephardic world, which tend to be more like fruit pastes than the chunky apple-and-nut mixture familiar to American Jews of Ashkenazi descent. I remember being surprised, when attending my first Sephardic Seder during my year living in Paris with a family of Jews, that the charoset came in a tube and looked like the filling of a Fig Newton. Since that time, I have grown to like Sephardic charoset, which certainly looks more like mortar—and that is, after all, what charoset is supposed to represent—than the Ashkenazi version. This may not be the charoset you are used to, but it is sweet, delicious, and well worth trying.

To make Sephardic-style date charoset, simply mix ½ cup (50 g) of chopped toasted almonds and ½ cup (60 g) of walnuts with 1 pint (475 ml) of date jam. If the mixture is too thick, you can thin it out by adding a splash of orange juice or sweet red kiddish wine. Refrigerate until needed.

DRIED FIG, APPLE, AND RAISIN JAM

I developed this recipe for Tu B'Shevat, which typically falls in January or February when most fruits are out of season. Thus, this jam relies on dried fruits, including the traditional raisins and figs, along with a jolt of citrus, which happily *is* in season during the winter months. The final result is a sweet, bright-tasting spread with a chunky texture almost like a fruit compote. It's perfect for stirring it into oatmeal, serving alongside a cake, or topping a bowl of ice cream.

½ pound (225 g) dried figs, stems removed and finely diced (about 1½ cups [225 g] dried figs)
2 medium apples, peeled, cored, and diced
½ cup (75 g) golden raisins
Zest and juice of 1 orange
Juice of 1 lemon
¾ cup (175 ml) water
¾ cup (150 g) sugar
½ teaspoon cinnamon
¼ teaspoon nutmeg

››› MAKES THREE 8-OUNCE (235 ML) JARS ‹‹‹

Prepare a boiling water bath and heat three 8-ounce (235 ml) jars.

Combine all of the ingredients in a large pot or Dutch oven and bring to a boil, stirring to dissolve the sugar. Once the mixture boils, reduce the heat to a low simmer, cover, and cook for about 25 minutes to soften the dried figs, apples, and raisins, stirring occasionally.

Once the fruit is soft, uncover the pot, raise the heat to medium, and return the mixture to a boil. Continue to cook, stirring frequently, until the liquid is reduced by about half and becoming syrupy, about 5 to 7 minutes.

Ladle the jam into the clean, warm jars, leaving ½ inch (1 cm) of headspace at the top. Bubble the jars and wipe the rims with a damp cloth. Place the lids on the jars and screw on the rings just until you feel resistance. Process the jars in a boiling water bath for 15 minutes. Allow to cool in the water for 5 minutes before removing. Store in a cool, dark place for up to 1 year.

LEMON CURD FOR PASSOVER

Because of the prohibition on leavened foods, most Passover desserts are made without baking powder or baking soda. They rely instead on beaten egg whites for texture. That is why practically every Seder seems to end with a sponge cake! Meringue-based confections, which do not even need wheat, are also popular Passover desserts.

All those sponge cakes and meringues leave a lot of leftover egg yolks. I remember being aghast when a friend confessed to me that she simply threw away half a dozen egg yolks every year when making her favorite Passover sponge cake. That is why I think this lemon curd, made with all egg yolks for an especially rich and silky texture, is the perfect Passover treat. Spoon some into yogurt for a kosher-for-Passover breakfast that won't leave you feeling deprived. Or serve it with that Passover sponge cake. But please, do not throw out leftover egg yolks ever again!

Note: Lemon curd may be frozen, but be sure to leave extra headspace at the top of the jars for expansion.

2 lemons

6 egg yolks

1 cup (200 g) sugar

*4 ounces (115 g) cold unsalted
    butter cut into small pieces*

▶▶▶ MAKES TWO 5-OUNCE (150 ML) JARS ◀◀◀

Zest and juice the lemons and set aside. You should have ½ cup (120 ml) of lemon juice.

Place the egg yolks and sugar in a medium, heavy-bottomed saucepan. Beat until light in color, about 2 minutes. Place the egg-and-sugar mixture over medium-low heat, and stir in the lemon juice and zest. Cook gently over medium-low to low heat, stirring constantly, until the curd is thick enough to coat the back of a spoon, about 10 minutes. Do not allow the curd to boil or the eggs will scramble.

Strain the curd though a fine-mesh sieve into a bowl to remove any pieces of cooked egg. Stir in the butter until melted.

Pour the lemon curd into clean and sterilized 5-ounce (150 ml) glass jars. Refrigerate until needed.

CANDIED CITRUS PEEL

Candied citron, or *etrog*, rind was a common Sephardic confection dating back to early modern times. Most of the candied citrus peel sold today is still made from citrons, but has a harsh taste and is laden with preservatives.

Better to make your own candied citrus peel using oranges and lemons, not citrons. Because most pesticide residue is found in fruits' skin, I recommend seeking out organic fruit for this project. Although this recipe does take some time, it will leave you with a large amount of candied peel, perfect for gift-giving, dipping in chocolate, or using in baked goods.

4 oranges, 6 lemons, or a
*   combination, scrubbed*
*   if not organic*
1½ cups (300 g) sugar, divided,
*   plus extra as needed*
1 cup (235 ml) water

Note: It is important to boil the peels several times to remove their bitterness and tenderize them. Do not skip this step.

▶▶▶ MAKES 2 TO 3 CUPS (ABOUT 250 G) ◀◀◀

For each piece of fruit, carefully score the peel into 6 wedges. Using your fingers, gently remove the peels, keeping the wedges intact. Repeat until all of the fruit has been prepared.

Place the peels in a large saucepan and add several inches (18 cm) of cold water. Bring to a boil and let cook for 5 minutes. Repeat the boiling process using fresh water. After the second boiling, scrape away about half of the white pith from the peels. Boil once more in fresh, cold water for 5 minutes. Remove the peels to a strainer and rinse. When cool enough to handle, slice them lengthwise into ¼ inch (6 mm) strips.

Meanwhile, prepare the syrup. Combine 1 cup (200 g) of sugar with the water in a large saucepan and bring to a boil. Add the strips of citrus peel and let boil for 5 to 7 minutes.

As the peels cook, place 2 cooling racks over 2 sheet pans (or newspaper) to catch drips. Remove the candied peel from the syrup with a slotted spoon and arrange on the cooling racks in a single layer. Let the peels dry for several hours until no longer tacky. Flip them over after about 2 hours to dry on the other side.

Finish the peels by rolling them in sugar. Spread ¼ cup (50 g) of sugar into an even layer. Working with one piece at a time, roll the peel in the sugar until all sides are coated. Add more sugar to the plate as needed. (If the sugar starts to form clumps, the candied peels are too sticky. Discard this sugar and allow the peels to dry longer.)

Place the pieces on cooling racks and allow to thoroughly dry for 3 to 4 hours. The peels can be stored for weeks in a plastic bag or container. If the peels were not dry enough when sugared, the sugar will liquefy when stored. Repeat the drying and sugaring process, allowing more drying time.

LEMON WALNUT EINGEMACHT

In the past, Ashkenazi Jews made a syrupy preserve known as an *eingemacht* out of their etrogs following Succot; some traditional communities still do so. This preserve was then served for the first time on Tu B'Shevat. It was traditionally eaten with a spoon while sipping hot tea.

Although this recipe is inspired by the eingemacht made from etrogs, I recommend using lemons instead. This lemon walnut eingemacht is similar to marmalade, sweet with a hint of bitterness. The addition of walnuts is typical for a Passover lemon eingemacht, but can be omitted if there is a nut allergy in your family. The final product is a pretty preserve, suitable for gifting.

1½ pounds (680 g) small lemons,
*   cut in half crosswise*
4 cups (950 ml) water
4 cups (800 g) sugar
*   (approximately)*
¾ cup (90 g) chopped walnuts

▶▶▶ MAKES FIVE 8-OUNCE (235 ML) JARS ◀◀◀

First day: Cut each lemon half into quarters. Remove the seeds and set them aside. Cut the quarters into thin slices and place them in a large, nonreactive Dutch oven. Cover with the water. Secure the seeds in cheesecloth. Add the seeds to the lemons for extra pectin. Allow the mixture to sit, covered, overnight.

Second day: Prepare a boiling water bath and heat five 8-ounce (235 ml) jars. Place a saucer in the freezer to chill. Bring the lemon mixture to a boil over high heat. Reduce the heat and simmer, uncovered, until the lemons have broken down and the liquid has reduced by a quarter, about 20 minutes.

Measure the volume of the lemon mixture and add an equal amount of sugar. If you have 5 cups (1 kg) of lemons, add 5 cups (1 kg) of sugar. Increase the heat to medium and stir to dissolve the sugar. Increase the heat to medium-high and stir frequently to prevent scorching. Boil the mixture, skimming off any foam, until it reaches 220°F (104°C) on a candy thermometer, about 15 minutes. (It may still look liquid, but do not overcook.) Remove the seeds.

Remove the saucer from the freezer and place a dollop of jam on it. Return it to the freezer for 1 minute. Remove the saucer and push the jam with your finger. If it wrinkles, then the jam is set. If not, continue to cook and try the test again after a few minutes.

Remove the pot from the heat and add the walnuts. Ladle the jam into the clean, warm jars, distributing the walnuts evenly, and leaving ¼ inch (6 mm) of headspace. Bubble the jars and wipe the rims. Place the lids on the jars and screw on the rings just until you feel resistance. Process the jars in a boiling water bath for 10 minutes. Allow to cool in the water for 5 minutes before removing. Store in a cool, dark place for up to 1 year.

What's an Etrog?

An *etrog*, which is also known as a citron, is a large, fragrant yellow citrus fruit with a thick skin and little pulp. Shaking one while reciting a special prayer is part of the celebration of the harvest festival of Succot. Etrogs (or citrons) are notoriously bitter. To make them into a palatable preserve required long periods of soaking to soften the thick rind. It also required large quantities of sugar or honey.

In addition to the difficulty of cooking with them, many of the citrons available in the United States are grown for ceremonial rather than culinary purposes; the growers use a lot of pesticides because the outward appearance is prized above all. That is why I do not recommend cooking with them. Perhaps a better use for your etrog following Succot is to stuff it with cloves and enjoy the fragrance.

JAFFA ORANGE JAM

Oranges appear frequently in Sephardic desserts ranging from baked goods to custards and even in some Sephardic versions of charoset. Sephardic cooks also preserve with oranges frequently, making jams, marmalades, and candies or *dulces*. Today, oranges, particularly the famous Jaffa orange, are an important export for the state of Israel.

While orange marmalade is more common, I prefer orange jam because it is less bitter and does not contain large pieces of peel. This is a simple and sunny jam that is best made in the dead of winter when citrus season is at its peak. Experiment with different varieties beyond the ubiquitous navel, from Cara Caras to blood oranges. While supreming the oranges is tedious, do not be tempted to skip this step. The membranes will make your jam unpleasantly bitter.

10 to 12 large oranges
2½ cups (500 g) sugar
½ cup (120 ml) fresh lemon juice
½ teaspoon cinnamon

Note: The peels from the oranges may be used for making candied citrus peel. To do so, remove the peels according to the instructions on page 91. Place the peels in a container of cold water and refrigerate until ready to use. The peels will keep for several days.

》》》 MAKES THREE 8-OUNCE (235 ML) JARS 《《《

Prepare a boiling water bath and heat three 8-ounce (235 ml) jars. Place a saucer in the freezer to chill.

Supreme the oranges. Carefully cut off the top and bottoms of the oranges. Use a small knife to cut off the peel and white pith from the sides. Then, working over a bowl to catch the juice, cut each orange segment away from the membrane in sections, and drop into the bowl. Continue until you have 5 cups (925 g) of orange flesh and juice.

Place the oranges in a large pot. The jam will bubble considerably as it cooks, so be sure to use a deep pot. Add the sugar and lemon juice. Stir well and set aside for 10 to 15 minutes so the sugar can dissolve. Bring the pot to a boil over high heat, stirring frequently. Once it boils, reduce the heat to medium and continue to boil until the mixture has become much thicker, reduced by half or more, and reaches 220°F (104°C) on a candy thermometer, about 25 minutes.

Remove the saucer from the freezer and place a dollop of jam on it. Return it to the freezer for 1 minute. Remove the saucer and push the dollop of jam with your finger. If it wrinkles, then the jam is set. If not, continue to cook and try the test again after a few minutes.

Add the cinnamon and stir to combine. Ladle the jam into the clean, warm jars, leaving ¼ inch (6 mm) of headspace at the top. Bubble the jars and wipe the rims with a damp cloth. Place the lids on the jars and screw on the rings just until you feel resistance. Process the jars in a boiling water bath for 10 minutes. Allow to cool in the water for 5 minutes before removing. Store in a cool, dark place for up to 1 year.

ORANGES IN SYRUP

Once they left the land of Israel, Jews throughout the Mediterranean began cultivating citrus fruits for religious reasons. Shaking an *Etrog*, which is a large citron, and a *lulav*, branches of three trees that have been woven together, is an essential part of the fall harvest festival, Succot. When Jews arrived in areas without citron trees, they set about growing their own.

The cultivation of other forms of citrus, particularly oranges for which citron trees were used as grafting stock, was a by-product of this religious custom. And indeed, hubs of citrus production today in Spain, Italy, North Africa, and the Middle East correspond with early Jewish settlements in those areas. Once Jews migrated to colder climes, where it was not possible to grow citrus, they began establishing citrus import businesses, again at first to meet their religious needs, but later for economic reasons. Thus began the long association of Jews and the citrus trade in the minds of western Europeans.

These orange segments in syrup are delicious eaten straight out of the jar as a light end to a heavy meal. They also make a lovely dessert topping. Try them with the Egyptian Semolina Cake on page 148. Because they are not overly sweet, you could even add them to a spinach salad alongside candied nuts.

6 pounds (2.7 kg) oranges
2½ cups (570 ml) water
1 cup (200 g) sugar
2 tablespoons (28 ml) lemon juice
4 cinnamon sticks

»»» MAKES 4 PINTS (1.9 L) «««

Prepare a boiling water bath and heat 4 pint (475 ml) jars.

Supreme the oranges. Carefully cut off the tops and bottoms. Use a small knife to cut off the peel and white pith from the sides. Then, working over a large bowl to catch the juice, cut each orange segment away from the inner membranes and drop into the bowl. Once all the segments have been separated, squeeze the membranes over the bowl so that all the juice may be used. (Supreming is tedious, but necessary, as both the pith and the membranes will cause preserves to have an unpleasant bitter flavor over time.)

Remove all the orange segments with a slotted spoon and place in another bowl so that only the reserved orange juice remains. Strain the juice through a fine-mesh sieve into a measuring cup; there should be about ½ cup (120 ml).

To prepare the syrup, combine the water, reserved orange juice, and sugar in a Dutch oven or large pot over medium heat, stirring to dissolve the sugar. Add the lemon juice and stir. When the syrup is hot, reduce the heat to low and slowly pour in the oranges. Stir gently to coat them in the syrup and allow to cook until hot, about 5 minutes. Too much stirring will cause the orange segments to break apart, so use care.

Place a cinnamon stick in each jar and then add the orange segments. Ladle the syrup over the oranges, leaving ½ inch (1 cm) of headspace. Bubble the jars, adding more syrup if necessary, and wipe the rims with a damp cloth. Place the lids on the jars and screw on the rings just until you feel resistance. Process the jars in a boiling water bath for 10 minutes. Allow to cool in the water for 5 minutes before removing. Store in a cool, dark place for up to 1 year.

Variation: Oranges in Vanilla Syrup
Omit the cinnamon sticks. When preparing the syrup, split and scrape two vanilla beans, adding the seeds and pods to the pot. When filling the jars, place half a vanilla pod in each jar.

BEET EINGEMACHT

Beet eingemacht originated as an Ashkenazi Passover confection. The only produce available in the cold climes of eastern and northern Europe at that time of year were the root vegetables that had been wintered over. With their natural sweetness, beets were the best candidate for being turned into a preserve to be eaten or given as gifts during that special time of year. (It's better than turnips at least.) Among the Ashkenazi Jews who emigrated to America, the tradition of making beet eingemacht for Passover persisted until the middle of the twentieth century when more commercially prepared Passover foods became available.

I know that beet jam sounds like a bad joke, but a very similar preserve called beet marmalade has become quite a trendy thing to serve with cheese. You can even find commercially made versions. So do not dismiss this funny-sounding jam out of hand. The earthiness of the beets is tempered by the sugar and lemon juice, and the ginger adds a bit of zing. It is especially lovely paired with something tangy such as goat cheese or yogurt.

Beets are a low-acid food, and it is critical to add bottled lemon juice and citric acid to this jam to make it safe for water-bath canning. You can find citric acid intended for use in canning online or at health food stores.

1½ pounds (680 g) beets, washed
and trimmed
1½ cups (300 g) sugar
3 tablespoons (45 ml) bottled
lemon juice
1 tablespoon (8 g) grated or
(6 g) minced fresh ginger
1 teaspoon citric acid

»» MAKES TWO 8-OUNCE (235 ML) JARS «««

Preheat the oven to 375°F (190°C, or gas mark 5). Wrap the beets in aluminum foil and roast until fork-tender, about 1 hour.

Prepare a boiling water bath and heat two 8-ounce (235 ml) jars.

Place the roasted beets in a food processor and chop finely but do not purée.

Place the beets, sugar, lemon juice, and ginger in a Dutch oven. Bring to a boil over medium-high heat, stirring to dissolve the sugar. Reduce the heat to medium and boil gently until thickened, about 10 minutes.

Ladle the jam into the clean, warm jars, leaving ¼ inch (6 mm) of headspace at the top. Bubble the jars and wipe the rims with a damp cloth. Place the lids on the jars and screw on the rings just until you feel resistance. Process the jars in a boiling water bath for 10 minutes. Allow to cool in the water for 5 minutes before removing. Store in a cool, dark place for up to 1 year.

Beets

Although humans have cultivated beets since ancient times, they did so originally for the greens. The root, which was longer and more fibrous than the version we know today, was primarily used for medicinal purposes. It was not until the early modern period that farmers began to grow the beet root for food as well as the greens.

Perhaps not surprisingly, the people of northeastern Europe, Jews among them, were the first to embrace the beet root as a dietary staple because it grew well even in cold weather and lasted for months in cold storage. The Ashkenazi culinary traditions use beets in a variety of salads, spreads, and soups, the most famous of which is borsht. The Sephardim add beets to their pickled vegetables to give them a distinctive pink color.

CHAPTER 2

PICKLES AND OTHER PRESERVED VEGETABLES

Pickled vegetables appear in both Ashkenazi and Sephardic cuisine, although not usually the *same* vegetables. The vegetables available to the Ashkenazi Jews in central and eastern Europe were typically root vegetables and other hardy species, such as onions, beets, carrots, cabbages, and cucumbers. These were pickled and fermented to last through winter not only to stave off malnutrition, but also because tangy pickled vegetables were a welcome contrast to the blandness and monotony of the rest of their winter diet.

When Jews from eastern Europe emigrated to America, they brought their fondness for pickles with them. Pushcart pickle vendors sold "sour" cucumbers, cabbage, green beans, beets, and peppers. One could buy a single pickle to eat on the spot or buy in bulk to take home. The ubiquitousness of pickles in Jewish delis, where they served to cut through the fattiness of pastrami and corned beef, cemented the association between Jews and pickles.

Sephardic Jews had access to many more vegetables than their Ashkenazi brethren, in part because of the warmth of the climates in which they lived, and in part because living at the cultural crossroads of the Mediterranean exposed them to vegetables from all over the world. Although pickling and preserving was perhaps not as important for survival for the Sephardim, there was still a robust tradition of preserving vegetables. These pickles were then served as part of a first course, or *meze*, and then again as side dishes during a meal. Even today, crunchy pickled vegetables remain an important part of Middle Eastern cuisine.

How to Serve the Pickles in this Book

For a Jewish deli-style plate of "sours," put out a spread of Deli-style Kosher Dills (page 104), Al Paster's Green Tomato Pickles (page 110), Polish-Style Pickled Beets (page 110), and German Pickled Red Onion (page 106). These mouth-puckering pickles would be the perfect accompaniment to a meal of corned beef, pastrami, chopped liver, or other rich Ashkenazi dishes. And if you're making a Reuben for lunch, homemade sauerkraut (page 112) is a must.

For a Middle Eastern meze platter, perfect for a cocktail party or as a first course for a festive meal, arrange an array of pickled vegetables such as Syrian Pickled Cauliflower (page 122), Pink Pickled Hakurei Turnips (page 123), Bene Israel Quick-Pickled Eggplant (page 118), and Middle Eastern Marinated Sweet Peppers (page 120). To round out your spread, offer traditional dips, such as hummus, tzatziki, or Annie Zémor's Matbucha (page 114), salads such as tabbouleh or fattoush, cubes of feta, and pita bread. With the addition of falafel, stuffed grape leaves, or kibbeh, this meze platter can turn into a complete meal, perfect for feeding a crowd. You can purchase any of the items that you don't wish to make at your local Middle Eastern grocer. But be sure to let your guests know that the pickles are homemade.

TRADITIONAL (LACTO-FERMENTED) KOSHER DILLS

If you are new to fermentation, this relatively easy recipe for traditional kosher dill pickles is a good way to begin. You do not need to purchase much in the way of specialized equipment. You can ferment your pickles in a gallon (3.8 L) glass or ceramic container or even several quart-sized (950 ml) Mason jars. Beyond that, you only need cheesecloth to cover the top of the container. Regular plates and bowls will serve to weigh the cucumbers down and ensure that they stay submerged in the brine. The oak leaves add tannin to the brine which helps keep the cucumbers crisp. I simply use oak leaves from a tree in my neighborhood and wash them well. You can also use grape leaves for the same effect, if you prefer.

Pickled cucumbers were one of the few vegetables that many old world Ashkenazi Jews ate. The typical flavorings for Ashkenazi pickled cucumbers are dill, which was common in Poland and Russia, garlic, and brown mustard seed. Garlic is the seasoning most commonly associated with Jewish cuisine. In common parlance, the term "kosher dill" simply means a dill pickle flavored with garlic, not one that is prepared in accordance with kosher dietary laws.

4 pounds (1.8 kg) pickling or Kirby cucumbers
1 head of garlic, divided into cloves

▶▶▶ MAKE 1½ QUARTS (1.4 L) ◀◀◀

Wash the cucumbers and trim off the blossom end (not the stem end). This end contains an enzyme which can lead to mushy pickles. Peel and lightly crush the garlic cloves.

3 fresh dill heads (or substitute
1 to 2 tablespoons [7 to 14 g] dill
seeds if you cannot source fresh
dill heads)

1 tablespoon (11 g) brown
mustard seeds

1 tablespoon (5 g) black
peppercorns

4 oak or grape leaves

BRINE

3 quarts (2.8 L) filtered water

½ cup plus 1 tablespoon (162 g)
pickling salt

Combine the cucumbers, garlic, dill heads, mustard seeds, and peppercorns in a clean gallon (3.8 L) container. Tuck oak or grape leaves around the cucumbers.

Dissolve the salt in the water to make the brine. Pour the brine over the cucumbers and spices. Use small plates or bowls to keep the cucumbers submerged. You can place a jar filled with water on top of the plates or bowls to help with this process. Make sure that the brine covers the vegetables by a few inches (10 cm). Reserve any extra brine in case you need to add more later.

Cover the mouth of the container with several layers of cheese-cloth secured by string or a rubber band. Place the container in a dark, cool (but not cold) place, such as a basement. Check daily to monitor fermentation process. The brine should begin to turn cloudy after a few days and you will see bubbles rising to the surface. Make sure that the vegetables remain submerged in brine. If the brine level gets low, add the reserved brine until the vegetables are covered.

If you see mold on the surface of the brine at any point, skim it off with a clean spoon. Replace the cheesecloth covering with a fresh layer. Begin to taste the pickles after 6 days by removing one using a clean utensil. When they no longer taste salty and are pleasantly sour, they are ready. This can take up to 2 weeks.

To store fermented pickles, skim any remaining scum or mold off the surface of the brine. Transfer the pickles to a clean and sterilized 1½ quart (1.4 L) jar and cover with brine. Keep refrigerated to halt the fermentation process. Pickles will last in the refrigerator for up to 1 year.

Fermentation

For centuries, pickled vegetables were staples in the diet of Ashkenazi Jews. Turks and Tartars traveling along the Silk Road from China introduced lacto-fermentation to Russia as early as the Renaissance and from there the technique spread westward. Fermentation, which required nothing more than salt, was an easy and inexpensive way to preserve vegetables and stave off malnutrition during the long winter. Vinegar, which was typically made from wine, would have been too expensive for most people to use as a preservative. Thus the reliance on lacto-fermentation. The tanginess of pickled foods, or *sours* as they were called, also added interest to an otherwise fairly bland diet. The main vegetables that Jewish women in eastern Europe pickled in this way were cucumbers, carrots, beets, and cabbage.

DELI-STYLE KOSHER DILLS

If you are not ready to dive into fermentation, you can make a version of the kosher dill pickle with a vinegar-based brine and process the jars in a water-bath canner. While not as traditional, these only take an hour or so to make, as opposed to two weeks, and they have the benefit of being shelf-stable. For pickles that I plan to process in a boiling water bath, I prefer to use dill seeds rather than fresh dill because I think they hold up better.

For packing these pickles in the jars, I leave the smaller ones whole and cut the larger ones into halves and quarters. I begin by placing a clove or two of garlic in the bottom of the jar. Then I add small, whole cucumbers and finally fill in the empty spaces with halves and quarters until I have packed as many cucumbers in the jar as I can without crushing or damaging them. It is also nice when opening the jar to have a variety of whole pickles and pickle spears to serve.

4 pounds (1.8 kg) pickling or Kirby cucumbers, washed and blossom end trimmed
3 cups (700 ml) white vinegar
2 tablespoons (36 g) pickling salt
3 cups (700 ml) water
6 to 12 cloves of garlic
6 teaspoons (14 g) dill seeds
6 teaspoons (10 g) black peppercorns
3 teaspoons (11 g) brown mustard seeds

▶▶▶ MAKES 6 PINT (475 ML) JARS ◀◀◀

Prepare a boiling water bath and place 6 pint (475 ml) jars in the water. Bring the water to a boil to sterilize the jars.

Combine the vinegar and pickling salt with the water in a saucepan and bring the mixture to a boil, stirring to dissolve the salt.

Remove a jar from the water bath and pack it with cucumbers, 1 to 2 cloves of garlic, 1 teaspoon dill seeds, 1 teaspoon black peppercorns, and ½ teaspoon mustard seeds.

Ladle the vinegar solution over the cucumbers in the jar, leaving ½ inch (1 cm) of headspace. Repeat with the remaining jars.

Bubble the jars and wipe the rims with a damp cloth. Place the lids on the jars and screw on the rings just until you feel resistance. Process the jars in a boiling water bath for 5 minutes. Promptly remove. Store in a cool, dark place for up to 1 year.

Note: Because these pickles are processed for less than 10 minutes, you must sterilize the jars before filling them.

Pickles and School Lunch

In the early twentieth century, those in the settlement house movement, which sought to educate and assimilate the hordes of European immigrants who landed in cities such as New York, tried to convince many immigrants to adopt more American foods. These reformers, some of whom were trained in the new field of domestic science, viewed sour, garlicky pickles as overly spicy and harmful, causing nervousness. They especially could not understand why Jewish children would spend their lunch money on a pickle and candy from pushcart vendors instead of more nutritious milk and bread.

The desire to eradicate this habit led a group of private citizens in New York to begin providing lunches to school children for only one or two pennies, which was the beginning of the school lunch movement that took hold after World War I.

GERMAN PICKLED RED ONION

Onions have played a starring role in Jewish cuisine since Biblical times and are mentioned frequently in Rabbinic literature. For Ashkenazi Jews in particular, onions, both raw and fried, were the principal seasoning for much of their food. It is impossible to imagine traditional Ashkenazi foods such as chopped liver, kasha, pierogies, and kugel without fried onions. Onions were so central to the Ashkenazis' existence that there are many Yiddish expressions that use onions as metaphors, such as *s'iz nisht vert tzibeleh,"* or "it isn't worth an onion." And the way you call someone a wet blanket in Yiddish is to call him *a bitereh tzibeleh* or "a bitter onion."

Pickled red onions appear across many cuisines, including German, Eastern European, and even Mexican. They are also a classic Jewish deli condiment used to garnish platters of smoked fish and bowls of chopped liver. The exceptionally pretty pink color and vinegary tang liven up bland, fatty dishes. What makes this version of pickled red onions distinctly Jewish is the use of sugar to create a sweet-sour combination, an important characteristic of German, and later Polish, Jewish cuisine.

4 large red onions (about 3 pounds, or 1.4 kg), trimmed and sliced

2 cups (475 ml) distilled white vinegar

1½ cups (355 ml) water

1 cup (200 g) sugar

1 tablespoon (18 g) pickling salt

12 allspice berries

12 whole cloves

3 teaspoons (11 g) yellow mustard seeds

1½ teaspoons black peppercorns

»» MAKES 3 PINTS (1.4 L) «««

Prepare a boiling water bath and heat 3 pint (475 ml) jars.

In a large saucepan, combine the vinegar, water, sugar, and salt and bring to a boil over high heat. Add the onions to the pan and stir to combine. Cover and return to a boil. Remove the cover and turn the heat down to medium. Boil the onions gently until softened, about 5 minutes. Remove from the heat and set aside.

Remove the jars from the water. To each jar, add 4 allspice berries, 4 cloves, 1 teaspoon mustard seeds, and ½ teaspoon peppercorns. Using tongs or a slotted spoon, divide the onions evenly among the jars.

Cover the onions with the hot brine, leaving ½ inch (1 cm) of head space at the top of each jar. (There may be leftover brine.) Bubble the jars and measure again. Add additional brine if the headspace is lower than ½ inch (1 cm). Wipe the rims with a damp cloth. Place the lids on the jars and screw on the rings just until you feel resistance. Process the jars in a boiling water bath for 10 minutes. Allow to cool in the water for 5 minutes before removing. Allow to cure for at least 2 days before opening. Store in a cool, dark place for up to 1 year.

QUICK-PICKLED BLACK RADISH

Mentioned in the Talmud, black radish is one of earliest crops cultivated by Jews. Both Sephardic and Ashkenazi Jews use black radish in their cuisine, but the highly nutritious vegetable was especially important to the Ashkenazim who could grow and store so few vegetables successfully. Raw black radishes appear in Ashkenazi salads, often combined with onion and dressed with schmatlz, or as an ingredient in chopped liver. In the *Encyclopedia of Jewish Food*, Gil Marks notes that black radish, or *ritach* in Yiddish, was even cooked with honey and ginger into a Passover eingemacht, which frankly sounds terrible.

Black radish has a distinctive coal-black exterior and a bright white flesh. They are larger than the red radishes we usually see—up to 3 or 4 inches (7.5 to 10 cm) in diameter. Look for black radish, which is sometimes known as Spanish radish, at farmers' markets in early spring and again in October. Choose firm specimens and avoid soft or squishy ones. The taste of raw back radish is quite peppery, but the pickling process tames the spiciness. They can also be substituted for turnips in many recipes. If you cannot find black radish, daikon radishes are the best substitute, but unlike with black radishes, you should peel them.

Here, in keeping with the tradition of raw radish salads, I quick-pickle black radish to preserve its crunchy texture. These radish slices, which will keep up to a month in the refrigerator, are delicious on buttered rye or pumpernickel, in salads, or as part of a relish tray.

1 pound (455 g) black radishes

1 red onion, sliced

1 cup (235 ml) apple cider vinegar

1 tablespoon (13 g) sugar

1 tablespoon (18 g) pickling salt

1 cup (235 ml) water

1 teaspoon black peppercorns

1 teaspoon dill seeds

½ teaspoon yellow mustard seeds

½ teaspoon celery seeds

»» MAKES 1 QUART (950 ML) ««

Wash the radishes well, but do not peel. Slice them thinly and place in a bowl of ice water until needed.

Sterilize a quart (950 ml) jar by filling it with boiling water and allowing it to sit for 5 minutes. Pour the water out and allow the jar to air-dry.

Combine the apple cider vinegar, sugar, and salt with 1 cup (235 ml) of water in a small saucepan and bring to a boil, stirring to dissolve the salt and sugar. Add the peppercorns, dill, mustard and celery seeds and allow the brine to cool to room temperature.

Pack the radish and onion slices into the sterilized jar. Pour the brine over the vegetables. Bubble the jar to release any air bubbles. Cover and refrigerate. Allow to cure for 2 to 3 days before eating. These quick-pickled radishes will keep for up to 1 month in the refrigerator.

PICKLED DAMSON PLUMS

Damsons are an ancient variety of plum, characterized by their small size and blue-black skin. Still popular in Europe, damson plums are little-known in the United States, but look for them at your farmers' market in late summer or early fall. You do not want to eat them out of hand, but they are excellent for baking and preserving. The flesh of the damson plum has low water content, which helps to preserve the fruit's shape in cooking, and it is naturally high in pectin.

Because they are so tart, damsons work well in savory dishes. It is difficult to separate the stones from the flesh. Thus, it was traditional to make preserves from whole, unpitted fruit, such as these spiced pickles. Pickled damsons are a delicious accompaniment to grilled and roasted poultry.

2 quarts damson plums (about 3 pounds, or 1.4 kg), pricked a few times with a fork
2½ cups (500 g) brown sugar
1½ cups (355 ml) apple cider vinegar
½ cup (120 ml) water
1 orange
2 cinnamon sticks, slightly crushed
½ teaspoon whole cloves
¼ teaspoon allspice berries
1 star anise

Note: Use regular-mouth pint (475 ml) jars for this recipe because the indent at the top of the jar will help keep the fruit from floating. You will likely have leftover syrup, which you can mix with seltzer for a refreshing, old-fashioned beverage known as a shrub. It is also delicious mixed into salad dressing or reduce it for use as a sauce.

>>> MAKES 3 PINTS (1.4 L) <<<

Preheat the oven to 275°F (140°C, or gas mark 1).

Place the plums in a baking dish large enough so they are mostly in a single layer. Set aside.

Combine the brown sugar, vinegar, and water in a medium saucepan. Using a vegetable peeler, peel the zest from the orange in long strips and add them to the saucepan.

Combine the cinnamon sticks, cloves, allspice berries, and star anise in a spice bag or tie up in a square of cheesecloth. Add it to the saucepan. Bring the syrup to a boil over medium-high heat, stirring to dissolve the sugar. Reduce the heat and simmer for 10 minutes to infuse the syrup with the spices.

Pour the syrup over the plums in the baking dish and cover. Roast the plums in the oven for 30 minutes.

Meanwhile, prepare a boiling water bath and heat 3 pint (473 ml) jars. When the plums are cooked, transfer them to the warm jars using a slotted spoon. Arrange the plums in even layers and pack as many as you can in the jars without damaging the fruit. This will prevent "fruit float."

Ladle the syrup over the fruit, leaving a minimum of ½ inch (1 cm) of headspace. This syrup tends to siphon out of the jars, causing them not to seal.

Bubble the jars and measure the headspace again, adding more syrup if necessary. Wipe the rims with a damp cloth. Place the lids on the jars and screw on the rings just until you feel resistance. Process the jars in a boiling water bath for 20 minutes. Allow to cool in the water for 5 minutes before removing. Allow to cure for 2 weeks before opening. Store in a cool, dark place for up to 1 year.

AL PASTER'S GREEN TOMATO PICKLES

Any Jewish deli worthy of the name will have a dish of kosher dills on every table. You know you are at an authentic deli if the dish contains kosher dills, half-sours, and pickled green tomatoes. Pickled green tomatoes were a favorite of my paternal grandfather, Al Paster, and he used to search through the barrels at the pickle store for ones with a slight reddish blush, which he thought had superior flavor. He was a bit of a character and always liked to worked an angle.

Green tomatoes are frequently available at farmers' markets in the fall for a good price. Many backyard gardeners will happily give them away close to the first frost, so ask around. Use smaller tomatoes because the wedges will fit in the jars more easily. Also, you can fit more wedges into regular-mouth pint (473 ml) jars than wide-mouth jars.

4 pounds (1.8 kg) green tomatoes, 3 to 4 inches (7.5 to 10 cm) in diameter, or smaller

3 cups (705 ml) distilled white vinegar

3 cups (705 ml) water

3 tablespoons (54 g) pickling salt

6 bay leaves

6 cloves of garlic, peeled

1½ teaspoons mustard seeds

1½ teaspoons dill seeds

3 teaspoons (8 g) black peppercorns

▸▸▸ MAKES 6 PINTS (2.8 L) ◂◂◂

Prepare a boiling water bath and heat 6 pint (473 ml) jars.

Cut the tomatoes into 6 or 8 wedges depending on their size. In a large saucepan, combine the vinegar, water, and salt. Bring to a boil over high heat, stirring to dissolve the salt.

Put the tomatoes into warm jars, arranging the pieces carefully, layer by layer, and packing them as tightly as possible without crushing them. Add a bay leaf and garlic clove to each jar as you pack them, as they will fit more easily than waiting until the end. Add ½ teaspoon mustard seeds, ½ teaspoon dill seeds, and ½ teaspoon black peppercorns to each jar.

Ladle the brine over the tomatoes leaving ½ inch (1 cm) of headspace at the top. Bubble the jars and measure the headspace again, adding more brine if necessary. Wipe the rims. Place the lids on the jars and screw on the rings just until you feel resistance. Process the jars in a boiling water bath for 15 minutes. Allow to cool in the water for 5 minutes before removing. Allow the tomatoes to cure for at least 2 weeks before opening. Store in a cool, dark place for up to 1 year.

POLISH-STYLE PICKLED BEETS

Beets played an important role in Ashkenazi Jewish cuisine. For example, chrain, a bright pink sauce made with horseradish and beet juice, is a traditional accompaniment to gefilte fish. And then there are pickled beets. Many cuisines from northeastern Europe—Scandinavia, Russia, Poland, the Baltic states, and Germany—have their own versions. Indeed, my mother, who traces her family back to Sweden, makes a version of quick-pickled beets for her annual Swedish smorgasbord.

Along with pickled cucumbers and sauerkraut, pickled beets were unquestionably a staple in the diet of Ashkenazi Jews. Because Polish Jews are known for their love of sweet and sour foods, I have made my version of pickled beets extra sweet with apple cider vinegar, sugar, and cinnamon. I like a heavily seasoned version of pickled beets myself, but if you prefer, you can leave out the spices or add different ones. Caraway seeds, for example, would make your pickled beets more Scandinavian, like my mother's version.

3 pounds (1.4 kg) beets, washed and stems and ends trimmed

2 cups (475 ml) apple cider vinegar

1 cup (235 ml) water

1 cup (200 g) sugar

2 tablespoons (36 g) pickling salt

4 cinnamon sticks

4 bay leaves

2 teaspoons black peppercorns

8 allspice berries

Note: If you buy beets with the greens attached, do not let those greens go to waste! They are incredibly nutritious. Wash them well in several changes of cold water and remove the woody stems. Sliced into ribbons, beet greens are wonderful sautéed with some garlic, and work well in soups, stews, and frittatas.

»» MAKES 4 PINTS (1.9 L) ««

Cover the beets with water in a large saucepan and bring to a boil. Boil covered for 20 to 30 minutes or until the beets are tender. Drain.

While the beets are cooking, prepare a boiling water bath and heat 4 pint (475 ml) jars.

As soon as the beets are cool enough to handle, remove the skins using your fingers or a paring knife. Cut smaller beets into quarters and larger beets into sixths. Then cut each piece in half, so you end up with 6 or 8 pieces for smaller beets and 10 to 12 pieces for larger ones. The beets will stain everything they touch, so be careful of your countertops and cutting board!

Combine the vinegar, water, sugar, and pickling salt in a medium saucepan and bring to a boil.

Pack the beets into the clean, warm jars as tightly as possible without crushing the pieces, leaving ½ inch (1 cm) of headspace. Add a cinnamon stick, a bay leaf, ½ teaspoon black peppercorns, and 2 allspice berries to each jar.

Ladle the brine over the beets, leaving ½ inch (1 cm) of headspace. Bubble the jars and wipe the rims with a damp cloth. Place the lids on the jars and screw on the rings just until you feel resistance. Process the jars in a boiling water bath for 15 minutes. Allow to cool in the water for 5 minutes before removing. Allow the beets to cure for at least 1 week before opening. Store in a cool, dark place for up to 1 year.

SWEET AND SOUR PICKLED RED CABBAGE

Sauerkraut is the most common form of pickled cabbage. For those of you who are not ready to dip your toes in the lacto-fermentation waters, here is a recipe for a vinegar-pickled red cabbage that is easy to make. It has a tangy flavor that is a delightful accompaniment to braised meats. The sharp taste also refreshes the palate when eating fried foods.

Cabbage was a staple food for Ashkenazi Jews, as it was for their neighbors. Cabbages not only grew well in the harsh climate and kept well but, of course, they are extremely nutritious. Many cuisines have a signature dish made with cabbage, from Korean kimchi to Irish colcannon to Hungarian stuffed cabbage. German Jews enjoyed cabbage, in sauerkraut, and they also combined cabbage with other vegetables and even fruits, such as apples. This pickled red cabbage has the sweet-sour flavor combination that Ashkenazi Jews favor. Try some alongside chicken schnitzel for a German-inspired meal.

1 head of red cabbage

2 tablespoons (36 g) pickling salt

3 cups (700 ml) apple cider vinegar

¼ cup (60 g) brown sugar

1 cinnamon stick

1 tablespoon (6 g) whole cloves

1 tablespoon (11 g) mustard seeds

1 tablespoon (5 g) black peppercorns

1 teaspoon celery seeds

Note: I recommend using regular-mouth pint (475 ml) jars for this project because the shoulders help keep the cabbage submerged.

>>> MAKES 3 PINTS (1.4 L) <<<

Remove the outer leaves and cut off the bottom of the cabbage. Quarter and cut out the white core from each quarter. Slice thinly. Layer the sliced cabbage and salt in a large bowl and toss to combine. Cover and place in a cool place overnight.

Prepare a boiling water bath and heat 3 pint (475 ml) jars.

Drain and rinse the cabbage.

In a saucepan, combine the vinegar, sugar, and cinnamon stick and stir to dissolve the sugar. Tie the cloves, mustard seeds, peppercorns, and celery seeds in a spice bag and place it in the saucepan. Bring the vinegar to a boil over high heat. Turn down the heat and simmer gently for 5 minutes to infuse the liquid with the spices. Return to a boil and then remove from the heat.

Pack the cabbage slices tightly in the clean, warm jars, leaving ½ inch (1 cm) of headspace. Frequently press down on the cabbage to create more room.

Ladle the hot brine over the cabbage, leaving ½ inch (1 cm) of headspace. Bubble the jars well and remeasure the headspace, adding more brine if necessary. Wipe the rims with a damp cloth. Place the lids on the jars and screw on the rings just until you feel resistance. Process the jars in a boiling water bath for 20 minutes. Allow to cool in the water for 5 minutes before removing. Allow the cabbage to cure for 1 week before opening. Store unopened jars in a cool, dark place for up to 1 year.

SMALL-BATCH SAUERKRAUT

Sauerkraut, or sour cabbage, originated in eastern Europe during the Renaissance, after traders from the east introduced the Chinese method of lacto-fermentation. Over the next few centuries, the dish spread westward, often carried by Jews, to Germany, France, and even England, until it became one of the most important dishes in all of northern Europe. Sauerkraut required so little to make—just cabbage and salt. It kept for months and provided an important source of vitamin C, as well as adding a jolt of flavor to otherwise bland diets during long winters.

In Europe, Ashkenazi families began fermenting cabbage and other vegetables in large barrels in the fall, around Succot. Once the fermentation process was complete, after two to four weeks, the finished sauerkraut was stored over the winter in a cool spot. It appeared frequently at mealtime, either on its own served with black bread or mixed in with noodles, potatoes, or meat.

Immigrants to America brought sauerkraut with them in the nineteenth century. The special kosher dining room at Ellis Island had both kosher dills and sauerkraut on its menu. Sauerkraut became a staple of Jewish delis and it is an integral part of the Reuben sandwich, an American invention which combines corned beef, Swiss cheese, sauerkraut, and Russian dressing on grilled rye bread.

1 medium head of green cabbage (3 to 3½ pounds, or 1.4 to 1.6 kg), as fresh as possible
Sea or pickling salt (avoid iodized salt)

▶▶▶ MAKES 1 QUART (950 ML) ◀◀◀

Begin by sterilizing a half-gallon (1.9 L) jar and a regular-mouth 8-ounce (235 ml) jar by filling them with boiling water and then pouring it out and allowing the jars to air-dry.

Measure out the salt into a small bowl, using a ratio of 1 tablespoon (15 g) salt per pound (455 g) of cabbage. For example, for 3½ pounds (1.6 kg) of cabbage, use 3½ tablespoons (53 to 63 g) salt.

Remove any damaged outer leaves from the cabbage and quarter it. Cut away the core from all four quarters. Finely shred the leaves with a large knife or mandoline. Place one-quarter of the shredded cabbage in a bowl big enough to hold all the cabbage. Firmly massage one-quarter of the salt into the cabbage in a large bowl. Repeat this process until all of the cabbage and salt have been combined in the bowl.

Set the bowl aside for 30 minutes to allow the salt to begin drawing the water out of the cabbage. Check the cabbage. A salty brine should be collecting in the bowl. Using your hands, squeeze the shredded cabbage, reserving the liquid, and pack it into the half-gallon (1.9 L) jar. Use a wooden spoon or other tool to lightly tamp it down and remove air bubbles.

All You Need Is Salt

Unlike most other vegetables, cabbage ferments in its own juice—so all you need to make sauerkraut is salt. Furthermore, you will not need any special equipment, just a clean jar and an out-of-the-way spot. The flavor and texture of homemade sauerkraut is vastly superior to store-bought and unlike commercial sterilized varieties contains healthy probiotics. You can also increase the quantity in this recipe to use more than one head of cabbage, as long as you maintain the same ratio of cabbage to salt.

After all the cabbage has been packed into the jar, add the collected liquid. The cabbage should be covered by the liquid. If it is not, you will need to add brine to cover.

Fill the small jar with water and cover with a lid and ring. Place this inside the neck of the larger jar; it will serve as a weight to keep the cabbage submerged. Cover the top of the larger jar with cheesecloth (to allow gas to escape but to prevent dirt or bugs from entering the jar) and secure it with twine, a rubber band, or a ring. Set aside out of direct sunlight in a room 55°F to 75°F (13°C to 24°C).

Once the sauerkraut has begun the fermenting process, you will need to check it every day to make sure the cabbage remains submerged in the brine. You will see small bubbles begin to form and collect on the surface of the brine. If there is any scum (white, yellow, or bluish growth), carefully scoop it off without stirring it into the liquid, and discard. The brine will become cloudy over time, and the odor may be pungent.

When it is no longer bubbling, the fermentation is complete. This process can take anywhere from 1 to 4 weeks, depending on the temperature of the environment. Once the sauerkraut is finished, store it in the refrigerator, dividing into smaller jars if desired. It will last for several months.

Note: To make additional brine: use a ratio of 1 tablespoon (8 g) kosher salt per 1 cup (235 ml) of water. Bring to a boil, stirring to dissolve the salt. Turn off the heat and let the brine cool to room temperature before adding to the cabbage.

ANNIE ZÉMOR'S MATBUCHA

Matbucha, sometimes spelled matboukha or madboucha, is a Moroccan dish of cooked tomatoes and roasted bell peppers seasoned with garlic and chili pepper. In the Maghreb, matbucha is typically served as part of the meze that precede the main meal. Israelis are tremendously fond of matbucha, and it appears frequently in restaurants as an appetizer.

Making matbucha is time-consuming, so many Sephardic cooks make it in large batches and freeze any unused portions. I have created a version that is acidic enough to be safely canned, so that you can make a large batch when tomatoes and peppers are in season and enjoy it year round.

Before serving, drizzle your matbucha with your favorite fruity olive oil. It makes a spectacular dip with warm pita. Try it also as a base for Shakshuka (page 134), or as a substitute for harissa in your Middle Eastern cooking.

*6 bell peppers (red, yellow, or
orange; not green)*
16 small green or red hot peppers
*12 large tomatoes, seeded
and diced*
8 cloves of garlic, minced
*1¼ cups (295 ml) apple cider
vinegar*
2 tablespoons (26 g) sugar
1 tablespoon (15 g) sea salt

»» MAKES 5 PINTS (2.4 L) «««

Preheat the broiler and place a rack in the upper third of the oven.

Arrange the bell peppers on a foil-lined baking sheet. Broil the peppers, turning two or three times, until charred all over, about 30 to 35 minutes. Place the peppers in a heatproof bowl and cover. Allow to stand for 10 minutes. When the peppers are cool enough to handle, remove the skins, stems, and seeds and chop them. Set aside.

Heat a skillet large enough to hold the hot peppers in a single layer over high heat. Blister the hot peppers in the skillet, turning two or three times, until charred all over.

Wearing gloves to protect your skin, peel the skin off the hot peppers and split open. Remove the seeds and dice the peppers.

Prepare a boiling water bath and heat 5 pint (475 ml) jars.

In a large saucepan or Dutch oven, combine the bell peppers, hot peppers, tomatoes, garlic, vinegar, sugar, and salt and bring to a boil over high heat. Turn the heat down and simmer until thickened, about 30 minutes.

Ladle the matbucha into the clean, warm jars, leaving ½ inch (1 cm) of headspace at the top. Bubble the jars and measure the headspace again, adding more matbucha if necessary. Wipe the rims. Place the lids on the jars and screw on the rings just until you feel resistance.

Process the jars in a boiling water bath for 15 minutes. Allow to cool in the water for 5 minutes before removing. Store in a cool, dark place for up to 1 year.

My First Matbucha

I associate matbucha with my French "mother," Annie Zémor. I lived with Annie and her husband Charles when I studied in Paris from 1994 to 1995 during my junior year of college. Annie and Charles were what is known in France as *Pieds-Noir*. The *Pieds-Noir* are the descendants of French colonials who lived in North Africa, often for generations, but had to return to France after the end of colonial rule in the late 1950s and early 1960s. Many Jews were among the *Pieds-Noir*, the Zémors included, because in 1870, France granted citizenship to the tens of thousands of Sephardic Jews who had been living in North Africa for centuries as a way to maintain France's sovereignty over the indigenous Muslim population.

Annie was a wonderful home cook, and it was she who first introduced me to North African Sephardic cuisine. I especially loved her matbucha, which she called *salade cuite de poivrons*. When I flew home at the end of the year, I actually packed some in my luggage, much to my father's horror. I still have a notebook from that year where I recorded several of Annie's recipes, from the couscous that she served to celebrate the end of Passover to this *salade cuite*.

Annie and Charles were the kindest of hosts and I was very fond of them. They fed me dinner every night, included me in their holiday celebrations, and welcomed all of my visitors from the States. I saw them again in 1999 when I returned to Paris and we caught up over a wonderful dinner. The next time I visited Paris, nearly ten years later, I had lost touch with them and my efforts to locate them proved fruitless. I suspect that Charles, who always had a cigarette dangling from his lips, has passed away, and I regret very much that we lost touch. They were the first exposure I had to the world of Sephardic Jewry, and for that I will always be grateful.

RABBI MAX'S PICKLED EGGS

This recipe is not like any of the others in the book, but I could not in good conscience leave it out. When I told my rabbi Max Weiss that I was writing a book about Jewish preserving, he immediately told me that in North Carolina, where he is from, Jews used to be known as "egg eaters" because they carried pickled hard-boiled eggs with them when they traveled. Intrigued, I researched this anecdote and learned that, indeed, the Cherokees were the ones who had bestowed this nickname upon itinerant Jewish peddlers who traveled throughout the American South and West in the eighteenth and nineteenth centuries. To keep kosher on the road, especially in places where pork was the dominant meat, these men either stuck to a vegetarian diet or brought their food with them, including beef sausage, pickled herring, and pickled eggs.

Eggs have a special significance to the Jewish people. The Passover Seder plate is not complete without a roasted egg. Associated with mourning in Jewish religious observance, hard-boiled eggs dipped in ashes are the final meal eaten before Tisha B'Av, the saddest day in the Jewish calendar.

Pickled eggs are a classic bar snack throughout the American south. There are many recipes, including sweet versions, spicy versions, and shocking pink versions made with pickled beets. This version is a little sweet with the use of apple cider vinegar, but it mostly sticks to classic Ashkenazi flavors, including dill, mustard, onion, and garlic. The vinegar gives the eggs a rubbery, but not unpleasant, texture. Pickled eggs make a convenient snack or a delicious addition to salads, sandwiches, or a classic English ploughman's lunch.

12 large eggs

1½ cups (355 ml) apple cider vinegar

1 cup (235 ml) water

1 small onion, minced

1 clove of garlic, peeled

1 teaspoon kosher salt

½ teaspoon yellow mustard seeds

¼ teaspoon dill seeds

››› MAKES 1 DOZEN EGGS ‹‹‹

Preheat the oven to 325°F (170°C, or gas mark 3).

Sterilize a quart (950 ml) jar by filling it with boiling water, draining it, and allowing it to air-dry.

Place the unpeeled eggs in the cavities of a muffin tin. Bake 30 minutes and then immediately plunge in an ice water bath to stop the cooking. When cooled, peel the eggs. Place them in the jar.

Combine the remaining ingredients in a small saucepan and bring to a boil over high heat. Turn down the heat and simmer for 5 minutes.

Ladle the brine over the eggs in the jar. Cover and refrigerate. Allow the eggs to cure for 72 hours before eating. The eggs will keep in the refrigerator for several weeks.

Note: I find oven-baking is easier than boiling for preparing large quantities of hard-cooked eggs.

BENE ISRAEL QUICK-PICKLED EGGPLANT

Whether fried, baked, roasted, or stuffed, eggplant is one of the signature vegetables of Sephardic cuisine. Indeed, in the seventeenth and eighteenth centuries, the British called eggplant "the Jew's apple" because it was so adored by the Sephardic Jews who were likely responsible for introducing the vegetable to their shores.

Eggplant has always been widely available, filling, and inexpensive: true peasant food. In the lean, early years of the Israeli state, for example, eggplant was one of the few vegetables widely available, much to the dismay of the recently arrived Ashkenazi Jews who had no idea how to prepare it.

Pickled eggplant is a specialty of the historic community of Jews in India, known as Bene Israel. This recipe has more of a Middle Eastern flavor than a South Asian one, but I love the idea that different communities of Jews have different takes on pickled eggplant. Two eggplants will give you three pints (1.4 L) of pickled eggplant, which may be more than you want, so feel free to halve the recipe. On the other hand, this pickled eggplant is so tangy and mouth-watering, three pints (1.4 L) can disappear in no time, especially if you offer some to guests. I like to put out these pickled eggplant cubes as part of a lunch spread.

2 medium eggplant, peeled and cubed

1 tablespoon (8 g) kosher salt

2 cups (475 ml) apple cider vinegar

1 cup (235 ml) white wine vinegar

1 cup (235 ml) water

1 teaspoon sugar

6 cloves of garlic, sliced

3 dried chiles

12 mint leaves

➤➤➤ MAKES 3 PINTS (1.4 L) ◄◄◄

Place the eggplant cubes in a colander and sprinkle with salt. Cover with a paper towel and weight down with a plate. Allow the eggplant to drain for 30 minutes.

Sterilize 3 pint (475 ml) jars by filling them with boiling water and allowing then to sit for 5 minutes. Pour the water out and allow the jars to air-dry naturally. Keep warm.

Meanwhile, bring the vinegars, water, and sugar to a boil in a large saucepan. Add the eggplant and simmer until softened, about 3 to 5 minutes. Using a slotted spoon, transfer the eggplant cubes to the jars. Add 2 cloves of sliced garlic, a dried chile, and 4 mint leaves to each jar.

Cover the eggplant cubes with brine, leaving ½ inch (1 cm) of head-space. Allow the jars to cool, cover them, and refrigerate. Allow the eggplant to cure for 2 to 3 days before serving. Pickled eggplant will keep in the refrigerator for several weeks.

Canning Eggplant

There is conflicting information on whether it is safe to water-bath can eggplant. The issue is the vegetable's density. Some sources question whether the heat from the boiling water bath will adequately penetrate to the center of a jar filled with eggplant. Yet, you do see recipes for canned pickled eggplant. I have decided to err on the side of caution and stick to quick-pickling eggplant. Because it does not spend any time in a boiling water bath, the eggplant retains its texture, which makes for a pleasantly firm pickle.

MIDDLE EASTERN MARINATED SWEET PEPPERS

A salad of marinated peppers is a classic Sephardic meze. This simple dish of roasted peppers, olive oil, vinegar, and perhaps some spice is sublime when the peppers are fresh and in season. But do not even try to make this dish with those anemic, and shockingly expensive, out-of-season peppers that are available all year long in American grocery stores. It simply won't be the same.

I prefer to stock up on sweet bell peppers in late summer and fall, when they are abundant and inexpensive at my local farmers' market, and prepare this recipe. Of all the preserved fruits and vegetables I have made in the past decade, these marinated peppers were my late father's favorite. They are wonderful on sandwiches and in Shakshuka (page 134), or served straight out of the jar, perhaps accompanied by Bene Israel Quick-Pickled Eggplant (page 118), as meze.

8 medium to large bell peppers (red, orange, or yellow; not green)

1 cup (235 ml) distilled white vinegar

½ cup (120 ml) bottled lemon juice

½ cup (120 ml) olive oil

¼ cup (50 g) sugar

1 tablespoon (18 g) pickling salt

Pinch of cayenne pepper

3 cloves of garlic, sliced

►►► MAKES 3 PINTS (1.4 L) ◄◄◄

Preheat the broiler and place a rack in the upper third of the oven. Arrange the bell peppers on a foil-lined baking sheet.

Broil the peppers, turning two or three times, until charred all over, about 30 to 35 minutes total.

Place the peppers in a heatproof bowl and cover. Allow to stand for 10 minutes. When the peppers are cool enough to handle, slip off the charred skin and remove the stems, core, and seeds. Cut the peppers into three or four pieces.

Prepare a boiling water bath and heat 3 pint (475 ml) jars.

Combine the vinegar, lemon juice, olive oil, sugar, salt, and cayenne pepper in a medium saucepan and bring to a boil. Remove from the heat. Pack the peppers into the jars and divide the sliced garlic evenly among them.

Ladle the brine over the peppers, leaving ½ inch (1 cm) of head-space. The jars will siphon quite a bit, so do not be tempted to leave less headspace. Bubble the jars well and remeasure the headspace, adding more brine if necessary. Wipe the rims with a damp cloth. Place the lids on the jars and screw on the rings just until you feel resistance. Process the jars in a boiling water bath for 15 minutes. Allow to cool in the water for 5 minutes before removing. Store in a cool, dark place for up to 1 year.

TUNISIAN HARISSA

Everyone agrees that harissa is a spicy red pepper-and-garlic paste from North Africa, specifically Tunisia, that Israelis love. But there is plenty of debate over what *other* ingredients belong in harissa. Should harissa have onion? Tomato? Paprika? Caraway? Personally, I prefer a simple harissa with peppers, garlic, cumin, and not much else.

Red cherry bomb peppers, which are similar to jalapeños on the Scoville scale, make a harissa that is fruity and not too spicy. If you cannot source them, use jalapeños, but reduce the weight to 6 ounces (170 g) of peppers because they are spicier.

This recipe is not acidic enough to be canned safely and adding more acid would change the flavor too much. However, harissa will keep in the refrigerator for months and it even freezes well. So make this recipe in the late summer and early fall, when hot and sweet peppers are readily available at the farmers' market, keep half, and freeze the remaining half until needed.

Harissa is extremely versatile as a condiment or an ingredient. Use it in your favorite Middle Eastern and North African dishes, as a flavor base for soups and stews, in a marinade, or as an accompaniment to grilled meat. Harissa is also delicious mixed with plain yogurt for a creamy, less spicy sauce.

4 red bell peppers

2 tablespoons (28 ml) extra-virgin olive oil, plus more to top the jar

8 ounces (225 g) cherry bomb peppers (about 12), seeded and chopped

12 cloves of garlic, peeled and chopped

¼ cup (60 ml) lemon juice

1 teaspoon cumin

1 teaspoon salt

▶▶▶ MAKES THREE 8-OUNCE (235 ML) JARS ◀◀◀

Preheat the broiler and place a rack in the upper third of the oven. Arrange the bell peppers on a foil-lined baking sheet.

Broil the peppers, turning two or three times, until charred all over, about 30 to 35 minutes.

Place the peppers in a heatproof bowl and cover. Allow to stand for 10 minutes. When the peppers are cool enough to handle, slip off the skin, and remove the stems, core, and seeds. Set aside.

In a large skillet, heat the olive oil over medium heat. When the oil is hot, add the cherry bomb peppers and garlic. Sauté the hot peppers and garlic over medium-low heat until soft and golden, about 10 minutes. Do not allow the garlic to brown.

Place the bell peppers, sautéed garlic, hot peppers, lemon juice, cumin, and salt in the bowl of a food processor. Pulse until the mixture resembles a slightly chunky paste, adding more olive oil if necessary. Taste and adjust seasonings.

Transfer the harissa into clean and sterilized glass jars, leaving ¾ inch (2 cm) of headspace. Add a layer of oil to the top of the jar. (Do not add oil if you are planning to freeze the harissa.) Store in the refrigerator until needed.

SYRIAN PICKLED CAULIFLOWER

Pickled cauliflower might be new to you, but it is a common breakfast food in Israel, along with cheese, hummus, labneh (yogurt cheese), pita bread, and crunchy salads of cucumbers and tomatoes. Like pickled turnips, pickled cauliflower is a staple of Middle Eastern meze spreads. It is a particular specialty of Syrian Jews, who are famous for their culinary prowess. This recipe is straightforward and simple, to highlight the flavor of the cauliflower. The beet is present mostly to add color.

1 large head of cauliflower (about 2½ pounds, or 1.2 kg) cut into florets

1 medium beet, peeled and cut into 1-inch (2.5 cm) cubes

2 cups (475 ml) distilled white vinegar

2 cups (475 ml) water

2 tablespoons (36 g) pickling salt

3 cloves of garlic, peeled and halved

1½ teaspoons black peppercorns, divided

▶▶▶ MAKES 3 PINTS (1.4 L) ◀◀◀

Prepare a boiling water bath and heat 3 pint (475 ml) jars.

Combine the vinegar, water, and salt in a large pot and bring to a boil over high heat, stirring to dissolve the salt. Reduce the heat, add the cauliflower and beets, and simmer for 5 minutes. Remove from the heat.

Add 2 garlic halves and ½ teaspoon peppercorns to each jar. Using a slotted spoon, pack the vegetables tightly into the jars, making sure to distribute the beets evenly. (There may be beets left over.)

Ladle the hot brine over the vegetables, leaving ½ inch (1 cm) of headspace. Bubble the jars well and remeasure the headspace, adding more brine if necessary. Wipe the rims with a damp cloth. Place the lids on the jars and screw on the rings just until you feel resistance. Process the jars in a boiling water bath for 10 minutes. Allow to cool in the water for 5 minutes before removing. Allow the cauliflower to cure for 2 to 3 days before opening. Store unopened jars in a cool, dark place for up to 1 year.

Note: I recommend using regular-mouth pint (475 ml) jars for this project because the shoulders help keep the cauliflower submerged.

PINK PICKLED HAKUREI TURNIPS

Turnips seem an unlikely candidate for pickling. But if you have ever eaten at a Middle Eastern restaurant, you probably have had pickled turnips without even knowing it. Those bright pink, crunchy pickled vegetables that are nestled into your favorite falafel sandwich are turnips. They are hard to recognize beneath that shocking pink exterior, which, by the way, comes from the judicious addition of beets to the jar.

Pink pickled turnips, known as *torshi left*, are a favorite among Jews from North Africa and the Middle East. In Israel, they are often served as part of a meze spread. I have modernized this classic Sephardic pickle to use not the large, slightly scary turnips lurking in the bottom shelf of the produce section, but rather the delicately flavored Japanese turnips, known as Hakurei or Tokyo turnips, that are available at farmers' markets in spring and fall.

Hakurei turnips are slightly peppery, but not at all bitter, almost like a radish. In fact, they are so sweet that you can even eat them raw as a snack or in a salad. Here, they make a tasty and eye-catching pickle. However you prepare your Hakurei turnips, do not discard the green tops! They are extremely nutritious and are delicious when sautéed.

2 pounds (910 g) Hakurei turnips

2 small or 1 medium beet

1 cup (235 ml) apple cider vinegar

3 cups (700 ml) water

2 tablespoons (36 g) pickling salt

4 cloves of garlic, sliced

2 dried red chiles

▶▶▶ MAKES 2 QUARTS (1.9 L) ◀◀◀

Sterilize 2 quart (945 ml) jars by filling them with boiling water and allowing then to sit for 5 minutes. Pour the water out and allow the jars to air-dry.

Trim the turnips and peel off the outer skin. Do the same with the beet. Cut the turnips in half and then cut each half into 3 or 4 wedges, depending on the size of the turnips. Repeat with the beet.

Combine the apple cider vinegar, water, salt, and garlic cloves in a small saucepan and bring the mixture to a boil.

Pack the turnips into the jars. Divide the beets equally between the jars and place a dried chile in each.

Ladle the hot brine over the vegetables, leaving ½ inch (1 cm) of headspace. Bubble the jars well and add more brine if necessary to cover the vegetables. Allow the jars to cool, cover them, and refrigerate. Allow the turnips to cure for 2 to 3 days before serving. Pickled turnips will keep in the refrigerator for several weeks.

ROMAN-STYLE PICKLED BABY ARTICHOKES

One of the best-known dishes of Italian Jewish cuisine is *carciofi alla giudia*, or artichokes in the Jewish style, which is a whole, deep-fried artichoke. This seasonal dish, which today is served as an appetizer in trattorias all over the Eternal City, originated in the restaurants of Rome's Jewish Ghetto, a place where food was scarce and residents endeavored to make the most of what they had.

Another way to prepare whole artichokes, especially the baby artichokes of early spring, is to pickle them. Homemade pickled artichokes are fresher-tasting and firmer than the mushy, marinated artichoke hearts you buy at the grocery store. Drizzled with your favorite extra-virgin olive oil, they are a wonderful addition to a salad or appetizer platter. Or, try them on a *pizza quattro stagioni*.

4 pounds (1.8 kg) baby artichokes (about 32 artichokes)

4 large lemons

3 cups (700 ml) distilled white vinegar

4 cloves of garlic, sliced

1 tablespoon (18 g) pickling salt

4 dried red chiles

▸▸▸ MAKES 4 PINTS (1.9 L) ◂◂◂

Prepare a boiling water bath and heat 4 pint (475 ml) jars.

Fill a large bowl with cold water and add the juice of 1 lemon. Remove the dark green outer leaves of the baby artichokes, stopping only when you reach the more tender, thinner, paler inner leaves. Trim off the tops and stem and slice in half. As you halve each artichoke, rub the cut edges with half a lemon and place in the bowl of water to prevent browning.

Juice 1½ lemons. (You will need ½ cup [120 ml] of lemon juice.) Combine the juice, vinegar, garlic, and salt in a large pot and bring to a boil over high heat, stirring to dissolve the salt.

Slice 1 lemon thinly. Remove one of the jars and place a lemon slice at the bottom. Pack the jar with artichoke halves, as tightly as possible without damaging the vegetables, and add 1 red chile. Repeat with the remaining jars.

Ladle the hot brine over the artichokes in the jars, making sure to include some of the garlic in each jar and leaving ½ inch (1 cm) of headspace. Bubble the jars well and remeasure the headspace, adding more brine if necessary. Wipe the rims with a damp cloth. Place the lids on the jars and screw on the rings just until you feel resistance. Process the jars in a boiling water bath for 15 minutes. Allow to cool in the water for 5 minutes before removing.

Allow the artichokes to cure for 2 weeks before opening. Store unopened jars in a cool, dark place for up to 1 year.

CRUNCHY PICKLED OKRA

Okra has been a favorite vegetable among Sephardic Jews since the Moors introduced it to Spain in the Middle Ages. (Okra originated in eastern Africa.) Once Europeans began eating tomatoes, after their discovery in the Americas, Sephardic Jews began pairing the two vegetables, much as people do in the American South. Sephardic cooks also pickled okra, along with many other vegetables, in a vinegar brine to serve as meze.

If you usually don't care for okra because of its slimy texture, I have good news. During the pickling process, the mostly hollow pods absorb the brine, which eliminates the interior slime. The end result is delightfully crunchy, free of slime, and will convert even dyed-in-the-wool okra haters. Look for small to medium pods, around 3½ to 4 inches (9 to 10 cm) in length, that will fit easily into a pint-sized (475 ml) jar.

*2 pounds (910 g) okra,
    stems trimmed*

*3 cups (700 ml) apple
    cider vinegar*

3 cups (700 ml) water

3 tablespoons (54 g) pickling salt

1 tablespoon (13 g) sugar

5 cloves of garlic, divided

1 lemon, thinly sliced

5 dried red chile peppers

2 teaspoons cumin seeds

»» MAKES 5 PINTS (2.4 L) «««

Prepare a boiling water bath and heat 5 pint (475 ml) jars.

Combine the vinegar, water, sugar, and salt in a large saucepan and bring the mixture to a boil over high heat, stirring to dissolve the sugar and salt. Once it boils, remove the brine from the heat.

Place a lemon slice at the bottom of each jar. Pack the okra into the clean, warm jars, alternating stem up and stem down to get as many pods in the jar as possible. Add 1 clove of garlic, 1 dried chile pepper, and ½ teaspoon cumin seeds to each jar.

Ladle the hot brine over the okra in the jars, leaving ½ inch (1 cm) of headspace. Bubble the jars well and remeasure the headspace, adding more brine if necessary. Wipe the rims with a damp cloth. Place the lids on the jars and screw on the rings just until you feel resistance. Process the jars in a boiling water bath for 15 minutes. Allow to cool in the water for 5 minutes before removing. Allow the okra to cure for 2 weeks before opening.

Store unopened jars in a cool, dark place for up to 1 year.

Note: I recommend regular-mouth pint (475 ml) jars to prevent the okra pods from floating above the brine.

PICKLED CARROTS TWO WAYS

Here are two recipes for pickled carrots: one with the typical Ashkenazi flavors of dill and garlic and another with the typical Sephardic and North African flavors of chiles and cumin. Both are quite tasty, and the carrot sticks standing up in the jars make for an attractive presentation. Serve them as part of your own meze spread, along with pickled turnips, cauliflower, eggplant, and marinated peppers, or alongside a favorite sandwich.

3 pounds (1.4 kg) carrots, preferably with the green tops on

2 cups (475 ml) distilled white vinegar

2 cups (475 ml) water

2 tablespoons (36 g) pickling salt

SEPHARDIC SEASONING

2 teaspoons cumin seeds

4 small dried red chile peppers

OR

ASHKENAZI SEASONING

2 teaspoons dill seeds

4 cloves of garlic, peeled

▶▶▶ MAKES 3 PINTS (1.4 L) ◀◀◀

Prepare a boiling water bath and heat 3 pint (475 ml) jars.

Peel the carrots and cut them into sticks 3 to 4 inches (7.5 to 10 cm) long. Bring a large pot of water to boil and blanch the carrots by cooking them in the boiling water for 60 to 90 seconds. Remove the carrots from the water and immediately plunge them in an ice water bath to stop the cooking. Once the carrots are cool to the touch, drain.

Combine the vinegar, water, and salt in a large saucepan. (You can reuse the pot in which you blanched the carrots.) Stir to dissolve the salt and bring the mixture to a boil over high heat. Once it boils, remove the brine from the heat.

Pack the blanched carrots into the warm jars as tightly as they will fit. Add seasonings: ½ teaspoon cumin seeds and 1 chile pepper per jar *or* ½ teaspoon dill seeds and 1 garlic clove per jar.

Ladle the hot brine over the carrots in the jars, leaving ½ inch (1 cm) of headspace. Bubble the jars well and remeasure the headspace, adding more brine if necessary. Wipe the rims with a damp cloth. Place the lids on the jars and screw on the rings just until you feel resistance. Process the jars in a boiling water bath for 10 minutes. Allow to cool in the water for 5 minutes before removing. Allow the carrots to cure for 1 week before opening.

Store unopened jars in a cool, dark place for up to 1 year.

Carrots in Jewish Cooking

Carrots appear in both Sephardic and Ashkenazi cuisine. They were far more important for the Ashkenazi Jews, who lived where so few vegetables thrived. Carrots not only grew well in the harsh climate and thin soil of northern and eastern Europe, but they also kept well in cold storage over the long winter, making them an essential part of the diet of Ashkenazi Jews. In a time when sugar was a luxury item, carrots were prized for their natural sweetness; for example, carrots cut into rounds to resemble gold coins is a traditional Ashkenazi Rosh Hashanah food.

While Ashkenazi Jews preferred their carrots cooked, Sephardic Jews often served carrots raw in salads or pickled as part of the spread of marinated and pickled vegetables, called meze, served at the beginning of meals.

NORTH AFRICAN PRESERVED LEMONS

Lemons preserved in a salt brine are a staple of North African cuisine. The addition of cinnamon sticks here is a particularly Jewish touch.

A small amount of preserved lemon in a dish goes a long way, and it is a versatile ingredient. Try a small amount of diced preserved lemon in grain salads, pasta dishes, with fish, in salad dressings, as well as in all your Middle Eastern–inspired tagines and stews. Preserved lemons also make an impressive edible gift.

6 to 7 organic lemons, divided

1 to 1½ cups (128 to 192 g) kosher salt

3 dried red chiles

2 cinnamon sticks

▶▶▶ MAKES 2 PINTS (950 ML) ◀◀◀

Sterilize a quart (950 ml) jar by filling it with boiling water, draining it, and allowing it to air-dry.

Cut a deep X into the tops of 4 lemons, but do not cut through the bottom. Place 1 tablespoon (8 g) salt inside each lemon.

Place a layer of kosher salt at the bottom of the jar, about 1 tablespoon (8 g). Place the first lemon in the jar and press down on it with the end of a wooden spoon to flatten it and release the juice. Layer ¼ cup (32 g) of salt around the lemon. Repeat with the remaining 3 cut lemons.

Juice the 2 uncut lemons and add the juice to the jar. The lemons in the jar should be submerged in a mixture of salt and lemon juice. If they are not, add another ¼ cup (32 g) of salt and the juice of an additional lemon. Slip the chiles and cinnamon sticks into the jar.

Cover the jar and store in a cool, dark place for 4 weeks, shaking several times a week to distribute the salt.

After 1 month, the lemon rinds should be soft and pliable. Remove the lemons from the jar and rinse off the excess salt. Place 2 lemons in each jar with some of the brine. Store the jars in the refrigerator, where they will keep for 6 months. To use, scrape off the flesh and use the rind only.

CHAPTER 3

USE YOUR PRESERVES:
RECIPES TO SHOWCASE YOUR
HOMEMADE JAM AND PICKLES

So often home food preservation enthusiasts find their basements and pantries overflowing with jars of homemade jam and pickles. I certainly have. We love the process of preserving, but sometimes run out of ways to use what we have made. That is a shame because preserved vegetables do more than sit next to a sandwich. And jam is useful for more than just spreading on toast! (However, if you want to spread jam on toast, I have a wonderful Challah recipe [page 138] that makes some of the best toast you will ever eat.)

This section of the book is designed to help you use your preserves with recipes for meals and desserts all of which incorporate a preserve from one of the first two sections of the book. Some of these recipes use jam as a topping; some use a vegetable preserve as the basis for a sauce; still others use fruit spreads as a filling for a baked good or dessert. Several are for traditional Jewish holiday foods such as Latkes (page 132), Hamantaschen (page 145), or Sufganiyot (page 146). With these recipes, your homemade preserves will soon find a place of honor at your table—be it dinner, brunch, or a special holiday celebration. No more overflowing pantries!

SWEET POTATO LATKES FOR HANUKKAH

Latkes, or vegetable pancakes, are the iconic Ashkenazi Hanukkah food. Most people think of latkes as potato pancakes, but you can truly make them with a variety of vegetables from carrots to zucchini. Indeed, potatoes did not really catch on as a staple food in eastern Europe until the mid-nineteenth century. The original Hanukkah pancakes were made with cheese, turnips, or other vegetables.

Personally, I like to make sweet potato latkes, so I can pretend that this fried food is somewhat healthy. But really sweet potato latkes have more taste than the regular kind, especially when seasoned with warm spices such as cinnamon, ginger, and allspice. You will need some flour to bind them together because sweet potatoes are not as starchy as white potatoes. These latkes pair exceptionally well with Cranberry Applesauce (page 68). For another way to eat latkes, combine 1 cup (230 g) of plain Greek yogurt with 2 tablespoons (30 g) of Tunisian Harissa (page 121) and use that harissa yogurt as a savory latke topping.

1¼ pounds (570 g) sweet potatoes, peeled
½ cup (63 g) all-purpose flour
1 teaspoon salt
½ teaspoon cinnamon
½ teaspoon ground ginger
¼ teaspoon ground allspice
Pinch of cayenne pepper
2 eggs, lightly beaten
6 tablespoons (90 ml) vegetable or other neutral oil

⋙ MAKES 16 LATKES ⋘

Preheat the oven to 250°F (120°C, or gas mark ½) and line a baking sheet with foil.

Grate the sweet potatoes on the coarse side of a box grater and place the shreds in a large bowl.

In a small bowl, whisk together the flour, salt, and spices until combined. Add the flour mixture and the beaten egg to the sweet potatoes and toss with a fork to combine.

Heat the oil over high heat in a large nonstick skillet. When the oil is sizzling, turn the heat down to medium-high. Scoop ¼ cup (55 g) of the sweet potato mixture into the skillet and flatten with a spatula. You can cook 3 to 4 latkes at a time, but do not overcrowd the skillet.

Flip the latkes when the underside is browned, about 2 minutes. Cook the second side for 1½ to 2 minutes until browned. Repeat with the remaining batter. Cooked latkes can be kept warm in the oven until needed. Serve warm with Cranberry Applesauce or harissa yogurt.

MATZO BREI ROLL-UPS

Matzo brei, perhaps the ultimate Jewish-American comfort food, is a relatively recent invention made possible by the advent of mass-produced, square matzo. To make it, either whole boards of matzo or broken pieces are doused with hot water until softened, mixed with egg, and fried in a pan. Matzo brei is often served for breakfast, or even dinner, during the week of Passover.

Matzo brei can be sweet or savory. Savory versions often include smoked salmon, cheese, or vegetables. Sweet versions are typically served with jam. Debates rage about what is the right way to make matzo brei, and the version I describe below, with whole boards of matzo cooked in a pan like French toast, is undoubtedly going to cause some readers to exclaim: "That's not matzo brei!"

Whatever you want to call it, this recipe, which came to me from Danielle Sandler, the administrator at my temple, is a delicious way to showcase your homemade jam. It makes a very sweet and special Passover breakfast.

2 eggs

¼ cup (60 ml) whole milk

1 tablespoon (6 g) orange zest

2 teaspoons sugar

1 teaspoon vanilla extract

½ teaspoon cinnamon

Pinch of salt

4 tablespoons (55 g) butter, divided

4 matzo boards (not egg matzo)

8 ounces (225 g) jam

Powdered sugar, for dusting

➤➤➤ MAKES 2 SERVINGS ◀◀◀

Bring 3 cups (700 ml) of water to a boil and gather 2 baking dishes that are wide enough to hold a whole matzo board.

Whisk together the eggs, milk, orange zest, sugar, vanilla, cinnamon, and salt in the first baking dish.

Melt 1 tablespoon (14 g) of butter in a 12-inch (30 cm) skillet over medium heat. Pour the boiling water into the second baking dish.

Add one matzo board to the dish with the water and soak for 1 minute. Remove and add to the dish with the egg mixture. Turn to coat the matzo.

Add the matzo coated with the egg mixture to the skillet. Cook over medium heat for 2 to 3 minutes. Turn and cook for an additional 2 minutes.

Meanwhile, place the second matzo board in the hot water and soak it for 1 minute. Remove to the egg mixture. When the matzo in the skillet is browned on both sides, remove it to a plate. Spread with 2 to 3 teaspoons (13 to 20 g) of jam. Carefully roll the matzo up into a spiral and dust with powdered sugar.

Repeat with the remaining boards of matzo, adding additional butter to the skillet before cooking each board. Serve warm.

Note: Vanilla extract is not kosher for Passover. During the holiday, use the inside of a vanilla bean instead.

SHAKSHUKA

Shakshuka, a North African dish of eggs poached in spicy tomato sauce, is a favorite homey break-fast or midnight snack among Israelis. I, however, like to make shakshuka for a quick dinner on those nights when there seems to be no food in the house. As long as I have a jar of Matbucha (page 114), a can of tomatoes in my pantry, and eggs in my refrigerator, I can have a homemade dinner on the table in less than thirty minutes. Because of the vinegar in the Matbucha, this sauce is quite sharp, so I like to soften it with a small amount of sugar.

With some crusty bread or pita on the side to soak up the sauce, shakshuka is a satisfying meatless meal. Of course, without the bread, shakshuka is a perfect kosher-for-Passover meal, and rarely a Passover goes by without me making shakshuka at least once.

1 pint (475 ml) Matbucha
    (page 114)
1 can (28 ounces, or 785 g)
    whole tomatoes
2 teaspoons sugar
5 eggs
Salt and pepper, to taste
2 tablespoons (8 g) chopped
    parsley (optional)

>>> SERVES 2 AS A MAIN COURSE <<<

Combine the Matbucha and the tomatoes in a large, deep skillet or sauté pan. Stir to combine and use a wooden spoon or your hands to crush the canned tomatoes. Add the sugar.

Bring to a boil and then reduce the heat and simmer until thickened, about 10 minutes. Make a well in the sauce with your spoon and crack an egg into it. Repeat with the remaining eggs. Cover and simmer 7 to 10 minutes until the egg whites are cooked but the yolks are still runny.

Remove the lid and simmer a few additional minutes, if needed. Season with salt and pepper.

Garnish with the parsley (if using) and serve.

GREAT-GRANDMA BESSIE'S CHEESE BLINTZES

Cheese blintzes are a traditional Ashkenazi dairy food for the festival of Shavuot. One rather poetic explanation for this tradition is that two blintzes laid side-by-side resemble the two tablets Moses received on Mount Sinai. Blintzes are an outstanding vehicle for homemade jam.

Jewish grandmothers will have you believe that blintzes are an enormous production to make. But it is just not true. Blintzes are only a production if you insist on making them by the hundreds, which, in their defense, grandmothers used to do. But contemporary cooks can simply make enough for dinner. And, in the era of nonstick crepe pans, they are not even particularly difficult. Blintz wrappers are sturdier than a typical crepe and are only cooked on one side.

I offer two options for filling. The ricotta filling is not traditional, but its smooth texture and sweet, mild taste is pleasing to all palates. The traditional filling, farmers' cheese, is fresh and soft with small curds. (Pot cheese, which is cottage cheese with some of the whey pressed out, is even more traditional, but can be hard to find.) You want a soft version, not a dry or crumbly one. Find farmers' cheese in better grocery stores; otherwise, quark (a fresh, drained German cow's milk cheese) or drained small-curd cottage cheese is a suitable substitute.

CREPES
1 cup (235 ml) whole milk

4 large eggs, at room temperature

1 teaspoon vanilla extract

1 cup (125 g) all-purpose flour

2 tablespoons (26 g) sugar

1 teaspoon salt

SWEET RICOTTA FILLING
15 ounces (425 g) whole milk ricotta

1 tablespoon (13 g) sugar

Zest of 1 lemon

Pinch of salt

▶▶▶ MAKES 8 BLINTZES ◀◀◀

To make the batter, whisk together the milk, eggs, and vanilla in a large bowl. Add the flour, sugar, and salt and whisk until combined and no longer lumpy. Cover and refrigerate for at least 2 hours or overnight.

To make the crepes, heat an 8-inch (20 cm) or 10-inch (26 cm) non-stick crepe pan over high heat. While the pan is heating, prepare 4 clean dishtowels or 4 squares of parchment paper to hold the cooked crepes.

Stir the batter to recombine. Once the pan is hot, reduce the heat to medium. Add $\frac{1}{3}$ cup (80 ml) of batter and immediately tilt the pan to swirl the batter to the edges. It should thinly coat the bottom of the pan. Cook undisturbed for 40 seconds to 1 minute until the edges are lightly browned and release easily from the pan and the center is dry.

Using your fingers or a thin, flexible spatula, loosen an edge and carefully remove the crepe to the dishtowel or parchment paper. (Do not use tongs, which may puncture or tear the delicate crepe.) If the bottoms of the crepes are browning before the center is dry, flip them over and briefly cook the underside and then add slightly less batter to the pan next time.

Repeat with the remaining batter. Layer the finished crepes between dishtowels or parchment paper. (Crepes may be prepared up to a day ahead and refrigerated.)

FARMERS' CHEESE FILLING

16 ounces (455 g) farmers' cheese

¼ cup (60 g) sour cream or plain Greek yogurt

1 egg yolk

Pinch of nutmeg

Salt and white pepper, to taste

Butter, for cooking

Jam or sour cream, for serving

Sliced fresh fruit, for serving

To make either filling, mix all of the ingredients together in a bowl.

To fill the blintzes, place one crepe, cooked side down, on a clean dishtowel or board and spoon 2 to 3 tablespoons (28 to 45 g) of filling just below the center of the crepe, leaving a border on the bottom and each side. Fold the bottom layer over the filling, then fold in each side, enclosing the filling completely, and roll up. Place the filled blintzes seam-side down in a baking dish. (These can be refrigerated at this point for up to 1 day.)

To cook the blintzes, melt 2 tablespoons (28 g) of butter in a 12-inch (30 cm) nonstick skillet. Place 4 blintzes in the skillet and cook over medium heat until lightly browned. Flip and brown the other side. Repeat with the remaining blintzes, adding more butter to the skillet as necessary. Serve topped with jam, sour cream, and sliced fresh fruit.

Note: Filled, uncooked blintzes can be frozen for up to 3 months. To freeze, spread the blintzes on a baking sheet; once hardened, they can be packed into gallon (3.8 L) freezer bags for storage.

Bessie Paster

My great-grandmother, Bessie Paster, was an accomplished cook and baker who was famous for her cheese blintzes, which she pronounced *buh-lintzes*. She was actually my grandfather's stepmother, his biological mother having died when my grandfather was fourteen. Grandpa Al called her Aunt Bess. She was a tiny woman, and everyone says she was very sweet.

When my parents were newly married and on their way home from visiting their respective parents on Long Island, they often stopped to visit my great-grandfather, Max, and Bessie, who lived in an apartment on Ocean Parkway in Brooklyn. Max took my father around the neighborhood to buy bialys and garlic sausages, those exotic delicacies not being

available in Washington, D.C., where my parents lived, at the time. They returned to the apartment for lunch, and Bessie always made her famous cheese blintzes, filled with pot cheese and topped with jam. She sent my parents home with bags of uncooked blintzes wrapped in waxed paper to fill their freezer. Between the onion bialys, sausages, and blintzes, it was a fragrant four hours in the car!

Great-Grandma Bessie died when my mother was pregnant with me, so Great-Grandpa Max hoped that they would name me after her. I admit that I'm grateful my parents did not name me Bessie; however, many years after his death, Great-Grandpa Max got a namesake in my nephew, the second Max Paster.

CHALLAH

Challah is a rich, eggy bread that Jewish families serve on Shabbat and holidays. For Ashkenazi Jews in eastern Europe and Russia, everyday bread was black bread, made with coarse rye flour, but even the poorest families used pricey white flour to make their challah for Shabbat. The traditional shape for challah is an oval, braided loaf, but on Rosh Hashanah, it is customary to make a round challah to symbolize the never-ending cycle of years and seasons.

This slightly sweet, golden challah is a worthy vessel for any of the jam recipes in this book. Because of the presence of eggs and oil, challah will last for several days without going stale. Any leftover bread can be used to make outstanding French toast or bread pudding.

4 cups (548 g) bread flour

2¼ teaspoons (9 g) instant yeast

1 cup (235 ml) water, approximately 110°F (43°C)

3 eggs, at room temperature, divided

¼ cup (60 ml) vegetable oil

3 tablespoons (39 g) sugar

2 tablespoons (40 g) honey

1 teaspoon salt

Poppy or sesame seeds, for garnish (optional)

▶▶▶ MAKES 1 LOAF ◀◀◀

In the bowl of a standing mixer fitted with a dough hook, combine the flour, yeast, and water. Stir to combine. Add 2 eggs, the oil, sugar, honey, and salt. Mix until a smooth dough forms, about 5 minutes.

Turn the dough out onto a well-floured board and knead by hand for 5 minutes, adding more flour to prevent sticking. The dough should be smooth and elastic. It may be slightly tacky to the touch.

Place the dough in a bowl that has been oiled. Cover with a clean cloth and allow it to rise in a warm place for 2 hours or until doubled in size. Punch down the dough and divide it into 3 equal parts. (I use my kitchen scale to ensure my pieces are of equal size.)

Roll each piece into a thin strand about 2 feet (60 cm) long. Pinch the 3 strands together at the top and then braid until you reach the end of each strand. Take the ends, pinch them closed, and tuck them under the loaf.

Carefully transfer the braided loaf to a baking sheet lined with parchment paper or a silicone baking mat. Cover the loaf with a clean cloth and allow to proof for 30 minutes to 1 hour until doubled in size.

Preheat the oven to 350°F (180°C, or gas mark 4).

Beat the remaining egg with 1 tablespoon (15 ml) of water in a small bowl. Brush the egg wash on the challah, making sure to get in the crevices of the braids. If desired, sprinkle sesame or poppy seeds over the top. Bake 35 to 40 minutes until golden brown. Allow to cool on a wire rack before cutting.

CHOCOLATE BABKA WITH JAM

Babka was a relatively obscure Jewish bakery treat until a 1994 episode of *Seinfeld* catapulted this sweet, yeasty bread swirled with chocolate, or less famously cinnamon, to wider fame. It has become so trendy in recent years that, in 2016, *Bon Appétit* declared babka "the new bagel": that is, the next Jewish food ready for mainstream success.

Babka, which means "grandmother" in Polish, originated in modern-day Poland and Ukraine. At first, women used their challah dough to make babka, and these early versions were filled with cinnamon, jam, and raisins rather than chocolate. This version combines chocolate and jam as a way to showcase your homemade preserves. Any fruit flavor that goes well with chocolate would work here, including apricot, orange, berry, and cherry. I recommend a smooth, rather than chunky, jam. Double-down on the flavor by enhancing the finishing syrup with a splash of liqueur or extract in the same flavor, such as Grand Marnier for orange or kirsch for cherry.

This recipe makes two loaves. If that is more than you need, wrap the second loaf well and freeze it as soon as it cools to enjoy another day.

DOUGH

4 cups (500 g) all-purpose flour
½ cup (100 g) sugar
1 packet (¼ ounce, or 7 g) fast-rising yeast
¾ teaspoon salt
Grated zest of 1 orange
1 cup (235 ml) whole milk heated to 120°F (49°C)
3 eggs, at room temperature
1 teaspoon vanilla extract
10 tablespoons (140 g) unsalted butter, softened

FILLING

Two 8-ounce (225 g) jars of the same jam or two different jams
2 ounces (55 g) butter, divided in half
(continued)

⟫⟫ MAKES 2 LOAVES ⟪⟪

Place the flour, sugar, yeast, salt, and zest in the bowl of a standing mixer fitted with the paddle attachment. Add the milk and mix until the mixture forms a shaggy dough. Add the eggs one at a time, followed by the vanilla, scraping down the sides as necessary.
With the motor running, add the butter 1 tablespoon (14 g) at a time until it is fully incorporated.

Switch to the dough hook and knead the dough, periodically scraping down the bowl and turning up the dough at the bottom of the bowl. Occasionally dust the bowl with flour to prevent sticking. (The dough will never clear the sides of the bowl the way a stiff bread dough would.) Knead until the dough is smooth and shiny, about 10 minutes.

Place the dough in a well-oiled bowl, cover, and let rise in a warm place until doubled in bulk, about 40 minutes to 1 hour. Alternatively, allow the dough to rise for at least 6 hours, or overnight, in the refrigerator. Divide it in half. Wrap the half that you are not using in plastic and refrigerate until needed.

In a small saucepan, combine 8 ounces (225 g) of jam and 1 ounce (28 g) of butter and heat over low heat until the butter is melted. Stir to combine. Set aside.

(continued)

1 cup (130 g) grated chocolate, divided in half

SYRUP

⅓ cup (80 ml) water

¾ cup (150 g) sugar

½ to 1 teaspoon flavoring, such as orange blossom water, rose water, vanilla, or fruit-flavored liqueur (optional)

Place the dough half on a lightly floured board and roll out to a rectangle of approximately 15 x 11 inches (38 x 28 cm). Leaving a 1 inch (2.5 cm) border on all sides, use an offset spatula to spread the jam and butter mixture over the dough. Top with ½ cup (65 g) of grated chocolate and spread with a spatula to mix the chocolate and jam. Allow the residual heat of the jam to melt the chocolate slightly.

Starting with the long end, roll the dough into a tight jellyroll and pinch the ends closed. Trim off the ends. Carefully transfer the roll to a cookie sheet lined with parchment paper and chill for at least 20 minutes.

Using a serrated knife, cut the roll down the middle lengthwise, exposing the filling. Turn the two halves on their backs so that the cut side is facing up. Pinch the two ends together and lift the right half over the left half. Then lift the left half over the right half. Repeat to form a twist.

Grease and flour two 9 x 5 inch (23 x 13 cm) loaf pans and line with parchment paper. Carefully transfer the twisted dough to a greased loaf pan. Repeat the entire process with the second half of the dough. Cover the loaves with a clean tea towel and allow to proof in a warm place until increased in size by 10 to 20 percent, about 40 minutes to 1 hour.

Preheat the oven to 350°F (180°C, or gas mark 4). Bake the loaves for 45 to 55 minutes until a skewer inserted in the middle comes out clean. If the top begins to brown excessively, cover with foil.

While the loaves are baking, make the syrup. Combine the water, sugar, and any additional flavorings, if using, in a small saucepan and bring to a boil. Remove from the heat and allow to cool.

Cool the loaves in pans on a wire rack. While the loaves are still warm, brush the syrup over the tops and sides. If syrup begins to pool on top, wait 5 minutes for it to absorb and then add the remaining syrup. Allow the loaves to cool completely before removing from the pans.

AMERICAN-STYLE CREAM CHEESE RUGELACH

Rugelach are a traditional Ashkenazi cookie that continue to be popular today. These flaky, delicate cookies are the perfect vehicle to showcase homemade jams and fruit butters. Traditional fillings were fruit preserves, especially apricot and raspberry, raisins, walnuts, cinnamon, chocolate, marzipan, and poppy seeds. But endless combinations of jam and fillings are possible. Some of my favorites include Peach Butter (page 60) or Apple Butter (page 71) with golden raisins and nuts; Fruitful Fig Jam (page 65) with chocolate chips; Plum Lekvar (page 62) with dried cranberries; and Sour Cherry and Almond Conserve (page 49) with dried cherries, cranberries, or chocolate. If you have nut allergies in your family, as I do, green pumpkin seeds, known as pepitas, make a terrific substitute for nuts and are even somewhat fitting: Sephardic Jews often snacked on pepitas, along with nuts and dried fruits, after Shabbat dinner.

Crescent shapes are the most traditional type of rugelach, but the cookies can also be made by rolling the dough into a log and slicing into rounds, which saves time when making large batches. Indeed, this recipe can easily be doubled if baking for a large crowd. I give you instructions for both shapes below.

DOUGH

1 cup (125 g) all-purpose flour

¼ teaspoon salt

¼ teaspoon cinnamon

Zest of ½ of an orange

4 ounces (115 g) cold, unsalted butter, cut into cubes

4 ounces (115 g) cold cream cheese, cut into cubes

FILLING

½ cup (weight will vary) jam or fruit butter

¼ cup (weight will vary) dried fruit, such as raisins or cranberries, or mini chocolate chips

¼ cup (weight will vary) nuts or pepitas (green pumpkin seeds), finely chopped

》》 MAKES 2 DOZEN COOKIES 《《

Place the flour, salt, cinnamon, and orange zest in the bowl of a food processor and pulse several times to combine. Add the butter and cream cheese and pulse several times until well broken up. Process the dough in short intervals, stopping to scrape down the sides as necessary, until large clumps of dough form. Do not let the dough form a ball.

Turn the dough out onto a cutting board and gently knead it into a ball. Divide the dough in two equal pieces, flatten to about ¾ inch (2 cm) thick, and wrap each portion in plastic wrap. Refrigerate for at least 3 hours and up to 2 days. (The dough may be made ahead and frozen; let it thaw in the refrigerator before baking.)

Preheat the oven to 350°F (180°C, or gas mark 4) and line two sheet pans with parchment paper or silicone baking mats. If using parchment paper, grease it lightly.

Work with only one portion of dough at a time, as it will soften quickly and become difficult to shape. Take the dough out of the refrigerator and let it sit for 5 minutes. This makes for easier rolling and reduces cracking.

2 tablespoons (26 g) cinnamon sugar (To make cinnamon sugar, combine ½ cup [100 g] of sugar with ¾ teaspoon of cinnamon.)

TOPPING
1 egg beaten with 1 teaspoon water
1 tablespoon (13 g) cinnamon sugar

TRADITIONAL CRESCENT COOKIES:

On a well-floured surface, roll out the dough until it is ⅛ inch (3 mm) thick and about a 12 inch (30 cm) circle. If the edges of your circle are ragged, trim them with a knife until smooth.

Leaving a slight plain edge, spread ¼ cup (weight will vary) of jam over the dough. Evenly sprinkle 2 tablespoons (weight will vary) of dried fruit or chocolate chips over top of the jam, followed by 2 tablespoons (weight will vary) of the nuts or pepitas, avoiding the center of the circle. Sprinkle 1 tablespoon (13 g) of the cinnamon sugar over the entire dough portion.

Cut the dough into 12 wedges for rolling into crescents. As if cutting a pie or pizza, cut the dough round into sixths and then halve each portion until you have 12 pieces.

Starting at the outside edge, carefully roll up each wedge into a crescent and place on the parchment-lined pan, with the end point on the bottom side. Do not panic if some of the filling seems to be coming out the edges; this happens and will bake with no problems.

Chill the formed cookies for 15 to 20 minutes before baking. Repeat the process with second disk of dough. When ready to bake, lightly brush the tops with the egg wash and sprinkle them with cinnamon sugar.

Bake for 20 to 25 minutes until golden. Let cool in the pan for 5 minutes and then remove to a cooling rack.

SLICED COOKIES:

On a well-floured surface, roll out the dough into a rectangle ⅛ inch (3 mm) thick and about 8 x 12 inches (20 x 30 cm). If the edges of your rectangle are ragged, trim them with a knife until smooth.

Leaving a slight plain edge on one long side, spread ¼ cup (weight will vary) of jam over the dough. Evenly sprinkle 2 tablespoons (weight will vary) of dried fruit or chocolate chips on top of the jam, followed by 2 tablespoons (weight will vary) of the nuts or pepitas. Sprinkle 1 tablespoon (13 g) of the cinnamon sugar over the entire dough portion.

Roll up the dough into a log. Starting at the long plain edge, carefully roll up the dough tightly and pinch the seam closed. Place on the parchment-lined pan, with the seam on the bottom side. *(continued)*

Refrigerate the entire pan while you repeat the process with the other half of the dough. After forming the second log, place it on the same pan, and refrigerate for 15 to 20 minutes.

Remove from the refrigerator, lightly brush the tops of the logs with egg wash, and sprinkle them with 2 teaspoons cinnamon sugar. With a serrated knife, cut into the dough at 1 inch (2.5 cm) intervals to form individual cookies, but do not cut all the way through.

Bake for 40 to 45 minutes until golden. Let cool in the pan for about 30 minutes and then slice the log all the way through to form individual cookies.

Note: If using a jam with large fruit chunks, such as fig or cherry, you may want to quickly purée it in a food processor for more even spreading or simply make sure the fruit pieces are evenly dispersed on the surface of the dough.

Why Is There Cream Cheese in Rugelach Dough?

The original European rugelach, which simply means "little twists" in Yiddish, were made with a yeasted dough. Rugelach dough made with cream cheese for extra tenderness is an American adaptation of this centuries-old cookie.

Cream cheese started to became popular in this country after Kraft began selling it in the late 1920s. It caught on quickly as more and more homes were equipped with refrigerators. During the Great Depression, cream cheese became an important source of inexpensive calories. At the 1939 World's Fair, Kraft handed out small cookbooks full of recipes incorporating cream cheese and after that, Jewish bakers embraced the mild, creamy spread.

Rugelach made with a cream cheese dough began appearing in American Jewish bakeries and cookbooks in the 1940s, and today we know no other way. Interestingly, in Israel, rugelach continue to be made with a yeast-risen dough in the European tradition.

HAMANTASCHEN

The traditional Purim treat is a triangular cookie known as *hamentaschen*. Hamantaschen have a bad reputation. All Jewish kids have been scarred by eating dry, tasteless hamantaschen filled with unpleasant prunes or not-very-sweet poppy seeds. By contrast, this recipe makes a buttery, crumbly but not dry cookie with a hint of lemon. It is filled with sweet, delicious homemade jam. Many of the jams in this book would work; I recommend an apricot jam (page 41), Plum Butter (page 62), Greengage Plum Jam (page 66), or, my favorite, Polish Strawberry Rhubarb Jam (page 30).

3 cups (375 g) all-purpose flour

1 cup (200 g) sugar

2 teaspoons baking powder

½ teaspoon salt

10 tablespoons (140 g) unsalted butter, cut into cubes

3 eggs and 2 egg yolks, divided

2 teaspoons vanilla extract

Zest of 1 lemon

8 ounces (225 g) jam or preserves

1 teaspoon whole milk

➤➤➤ MAKES 2 DOZEN COOKIES ◀◀◀

Place the flour, sugar, baking powder, and salt in the bowl of a food processor and pulse a few times to combine. Add the butter and process for a few seconds until the mixture resembles coarse crumbs.

In a separate bowl, whisk together 2 of the eggs, the egg yolks, vanilla, and lemon zest. Add the egg mixture to the food processor and process for 30 seconds. It will still be somewhat dry and crumbly.

Turn the dough out onto a floured surface, gather into a ball, and knead until it comes together. Divide it in half and form into two discs. Wrap each in plastic wrap and refrigerate for several hours or overnight.

To make the cookies, remove one of the discs from the refrigerator and let the dough warm up slightly to make it easier to roll out.

Preheat the oven to 350°F (180°C, or gas mark 4). Line 2 baking sheets with silicone baking mats or parchment paper.

Roll out the dough on a well-floured surface to ¼ inch (6 mm) thick. Using a 4 inch (10 cm) round cookie cutter or a round drinking glass, cut out circles and place them on the lined cookie sheets. Gather up the scraps of dough and re-roll to make more circles.

To fill the cookies, spoon 1 teaspoon of jam or preserves in the center of the dough circle.

To create the triangle shape, fold one side of the cookie in so that the edge comes to the middle of the jam filling. Fold the second side in the same way and so that it partially covers the first side. Fold the remaining side up and in so that it overlaps the other two sides. Chill for at least 10 minutes before baking. Repeat with the remaining disc.

Make an egg wash of the remaining egg beaten with the milk. Brush the outside of the cookies with egg wash with a pastry brush. Bake for 15 minutes or so until the cookies are golden brown. Cool on a wire rack.

ISRAELI JELLY DOUGHNUTS (SUFGANIYOT)

These yeast-risen, jam-filled, fried pastries originated in eastern Europe. A Czech friend claims that my sufganiyot look exactly like the *koblihw* she ate growing up. Others say that they resemble a Polish *paczki*. Both of those pastries, special indulgences for Fat Tuesday, the day before Ash Wednesday and the beginning of Lent, became common in the nineteenth century after sugar was inexpensive enough for common people to afford regularly. Paczkis and their brethren were typically fried in lard. Jews from the region adopted the notion of a doughnut fried in fat, but used oil or schmaltz instead.

Today, sufganiyot are known as the food most associated with the festival of Hanukkah in Israel. Israelis go mad for sufganiyot during Hanukkah, with hundreds of thousands of the pastries sold throughout the country. Sufganiyot are a fitting Hanukkah food because, like latkes, they are fried in oil.

I think of sufganiyot as a way to showcase homemade jams. Select smooth jams, not chunky ones which can get stuck in the piping bag. Apricot and raspberry are the most traditional. Of the recipes in this book, Polish Strawberry Rhubarb Jam (page 30) or Raspberry Red Currant Jam (page 34) are both excellent choices. Lemon Curd (page 98) would also be a fun twist.

2¼ teaspoons (9 g) active
    dry yeast
½ cup (120 ml) whole milk, heated
    to 120°F (49°C)
2½ cups (313 g) all-purpose flour
¼ cup (50 g) sugar
Pinch of salt
¼ teaspoon cinnamon
2 eggs, at room temperature
1 teaspoon vanilla extract
2 tablespoons (28 g) butter,
    softened
12 ounces (340 g) jam
64 ounces (1.8 L) vegetable or
    other neutral oil for frying

⟫⟫⟫ MAKES 12 TO 14 DOUGHNUTS ⟪⟪⟪

Mix the yeast, warm milk, and a pinch of sugar together in a small bowl. Allow to rest until foamy, about 10 minutes.

In the bowl of a standing mixer or large mixing bowl, whisk together the flour, sugar, salt, and cinnamon. Add the yeast mixture and start to mix using the paddle attachment. Add the eggs one at a time and then add the vanilla, followed by the butter. Continue to mix until the dough comes together.

Switch to the dough hook and knead. Alternatively, turn out onto a well-floured board and knead by hand until the dough is smooth and elastic, about 5 minutes.

Place the dough in an oiled bowl and allow to rise in a warm place until doubled in size, about 1 hour. Punch down the dough and turn out onto a well-floured board. Roll out until it is ½ to ¼ inch (1 to 10 .6 cm) thick. The dough may spring back. If it does, allow it to rest for 5 minutes and continue.

Using a round cookie cutter 3 inches (7.5 cm) in diameter, cut out as many circles of dough as you can. Gather the scraps and roll out again. Cut as many more circles as you can, about 12 to 14 total. Place the circles on a baking sheet lined with parchment paper. Cover with a clean towel and allow to proof for 30 minutes.

Heat several inches (18 cm) of oil in a deep, heavy saucepan until it reaches 360°F (182°C) on a candy thermometer. It's critical to reach and maintain this temperature so that the doughnuts cook all the way through but do not burn. In addition, maintaining the correct temperature will ensure that the doughnuts do not absorb too much oil and become greasy.

Add 4 doughnuts to the hot oil. They will puff up immediately. Flip the doughnuts after 1 minute. The doughnuts will brown quickly and some will flip over by themselves. Cook until both sides are golden brown, about 2 minutes total. Drain on paper towels. Repeat with the remaining doughnuts.

When the doughnuts are cool enough to handle, poke a hole in one end with a skewer and move the skewer around in a circle inside the doughnut to create space for the jam. Take care not to poke additional holes in the doughnut.

Using a piping bag outfitted with a ¼-inch (6 mm) tip, pipe the jam in the hole just until it starts to spill out. Repeat with the remaining sufganiyot. Dust with powdered sugar and serve.

BASBOUSA (EGYPTIAN SEMOLINA CAKE)

Throughout the Middle East you encounter cakes, often served in diamond-shaped pieces that are made with semolina flour and drenched in a sugar syrup for sweetness and moisture. Some versions contain eggs, some yogurt, some coconut, and some almonds, but all share the two elements of semolina and syrup. This very same cake, albeit called a number of different things, such as tishpishti, revani, or namoura, also appears in North Africa, Turkey, Greece, and the Balkans. But the cake traces its origins to Sephardic Jews from Egypt. Today, in Israel, basbousa made with yogurt is a popular dessert at Shavout, when it is traditional to eat dairy foods; a nondairy version is served on Rosh Hashanah, when everyone strives to begin the new year on a sweet note.

Semolina is a form of durum, an ancient species of wheat that has remained popular in the Middle East and Mediterranean for making couscous, bulgur, pastries, and puddings. It has a pale yellow color and slightly grainier texture than regular flour. Here, the semolina gives the cake a crumbly texture, a slightly crunchy exterior, and a nuttiness that is a pleasing contrast to the sweetness of the syrup.

You can make a sugar syrup from scratch to douse your cake or use the Rose Petal Syrup recipe on page 35 of this book. Another idea is to open a jar of the Oranges in Syrup (page 96) and use the syrup as the base for a citrusy syrup and garnish the cake with the reserved orange segments.

SYRUP

1½ cups (300 g) sugar

1½ cups (355 ml) water

2 tablespoons (28 ml) fresh
    lemon juice

2 to 3 drops of orange blossom
    water (optional)

OR

1 jar of Oranges in Syrup
    (page 96)

¾ cup (175 ml) water

1 cup (200 g) sugar

»» MAKES 1 CAKE ««

Preheat the oven to 350°F (180°C, or gas mark 4) and grease a 9 inch (23 cm) round cake pan.

If making the syrup from scratch, combine the sugar and water in a small saucepan and bring to a boil over high heat, stirring to dissolve the sugar. Add the lemon juice and the orange blossom water (if using), reduce the heat to medium, and boil for 5 minutes. Remove from the heat and allow to cool.

If using the Oranges in Syrup, pour the syrup from the jar into a saucepan, reserving the oranges to garnish the cake. Add the water and sugar to the syrup in the pan. Bring to a boil over high heat, stirring to dissolve the sugar. Reduce the heat to medium and boil for 5 minutes. Remove from the heat and allow to cool.

CAKE

2 cups (336 g) semolina flour

1 teaspoon baking powder

½ teaspoon baking soda

½ teaspoon salt

3 eggs

½ cup (100 g) sugar

1 cup (235 ml) vegetable oil

1 teaspoon vanilla extract

1 cup (230 g) plain whole milk yogurt

Zest of 1 orange

To make the cake, whisk together the semolina, baking powder, baking soda, and salt in a small bowl. Set aside.

Combine the eggs and sugar in the bowl of a standing mixer and beat on medium speed until light and fluffy, about 3 minutes. With the mixer running, slowly pour in the oil and mix until combined. Add the vanilla. Add the yogurt and mix until combined. Gradually add the dry ingredients and mix just until combined. Add the orange zest and fold it in.

Pour the batter into the prepared pan and bake until the edges begin to pull away from the sides of the pan and a skewer inserted in the middle comes out clean, about 40 to 45 minutes.

While the cake is still hot, slowly pour the syrup over the top, pausing periodically to allow the cake to absorb the syrup before adding more. Cool the cake on a wire rack before removing from pan. If using Oranges in Syrup, serve with the reserved orange segments on the side.

ACKNOWLEDGMENTS

I would like to thank all of the people who created this book with me. Most significantly, Genevieve Boehme either tested or helped to develop almost every recipe in this book, and I could not have completed it without her help. Writing books can be a lonely business, so I was grateful to have a collaborator on this project, especially one so enthusiastic and dedicated.

Leigh Olson was another wonderful collaborator. Not only did Leigh style and capture all of the beautiful images in this book—despite the uncooperative Seattle weather—she also hosted me during the photo shoot. Thanks also to Rose McAvoy, who assisted with the prop styling, and Eric Biermann for outstanding technical and culinary support.

Thanks to Max Weiss, the rabbi of Oak Park Temple, which has been my Jewish home for the past decade, for reviewing the descriptions of the Jewish holidays and other aspects of Jewish life in this book. Any mistakes on those subjects are entirely my own.

My father-in-law, professor Joe Regenstein, a food scientist and internationally recognized expert on *kashrut*, assisted me with the overview of the Jewish dietary laws, for which I am extremely grateful. I alone am to blame for any mistakes in those paragraphs. Thanks also to my mother-in-law, Carrie Regenstein, for helping with child care at critical moments in the preparation of this manuscript.

Although I have lost touch with them, I would like to acknowledge Annie and Charles Zémor, my Parisian family during my junior year abroad in 1994 and 1995. They were incredibly generous hosts and my first introduction to the cuisine and culture of Sephardic Jews, which has fascinated me ever since.

To my literary agent, Clare Pelino, thanks for believing in this project ever since I first mentioned it in 2014 and for always being either patient or aggressive as the situation warrants.

Thanks to the team at Harvard Common Press and Quarto, including Dan Rosenberg, Heather Godin, and Cara Connors, for their hard work in turning a bare manuscript into a stunning book. Thanks also to Jenna Patton for incredibly good-natured and professional copyediting.

I would like to thank the staff at the River Forest Public Library for fielding my frequent and sometimes challenging interlibrary loan requests and for providing me with such a comfortable place to write.

To my aunt Ann Brody Cove, the best Jewish cook I know, thanks for sharing some of her family memories.

Thanks to my mother Gail Kern Paster, the best writer I know, for the information about early modern medicine and for her generous and enthusiastic support.

Boundless love and gratitude to my husband, Elliot Regenstein, and my children, Zoe and Jamie Regenstein, for their support, love, and patience. I am very proud of the Jewish life we have created together.

SELECTED BIBLIOGRAPHY

BOOKS

Abrahams, Bernard. *Mayne zibetsik yor: otobiyografye*. Johanesburg: Kayor, 1953.

Cooper, John. *Eat and Be Satisfied: A Social History of Jewish Food*. Northvale, NJ: Jason Aronson Inc., 1993.

Dweck, Poopa. *Aromas of Aleppo: The Legendary Cuisine of Syrian Jews*. New York: Ecco, 2007.

Gur, Janna. *Jewish Soul Food: From Minsk to Marrakesh: More than 100 Unforgettable Dishes Updated for Today's Kitchen*. New York: Schocken, 2014.

Harvey, William. *The Anatomical Lectures of William Harvey: Prelectiones Anatomiae Universalis de Musculis*. E. & S. Livingstone, 1964.

Levy, Esther. *The First Jewish-American Cookbook (1871)*. Mineola, NY: Dover Publications, 2004.

Marks, Gil. *Encyclopedia of Jewish Food*. Hoboken, NJ: Wiley, 2010.

Nadell, Pamela Susan. *American Jewish Women's History: A Reader*. New York: NYU Press, 2003.

Nathan, Joan. *Jewish Cooking in America*. New York: A. Knopf, 1994.

Roden, Claudia. *The Book of Jewish Food: An Odyssey from Samarkand to New York*. New York: Knopf, 1996.

Rose, Evelyn. *The New Complete International Jewish Cookbook*. New York: Carroll & Graf, 1993.

Saltsman, Amelia. *The Seasonal Jewish Kitchen: A Fresh Take on Tradition*. New York: Sterling Epicure, 2015.

Ziegelman, Jane. *97 Orchard: An Edible History of Five Immigrant Families in One New York Tenement*. New York: Smithsonian Books /HarperCollins, 2010.

Zusman, Michael C., and Nick Zukin. *The Artisan Jewish Deli at Home*. Kansas City: Andrews McMeel Publishing, LLC, 2013.

ARTICLES

Julia Moskin, "Cooking Defines Sephardic Jews at Sukkot," *New York Times*, October 11, 2006.

Toby Sonneman, "After Sukkot Is Over, Don't Discard That Etrog," *Tablet*, September 28, 2012.

ABOUT THE AUTHOR

Emily Paster grew up in Washington, D.C., in an interfaith family that was blessed with many outstanding cooks. A graduate of Princeton University and the University of Michigan Law School, Emily redirected her career from law to food after the birth of her second child. She is the writer and photographer behind the website *West of the Loop*, which has been called "a family food blog to savor." As the founder of the Chicago Food Swap, a community event where handmade foods are bartered and exchanged, Emily is a leader in the national food swap movement. She is the author of *Food Swap: Specialty Recipes for Bartering, Sharing & Giving*. She teaches and speaks on garden-to-table cooking, canning, and fermentation throughout the country. *The Joys of Jewish Preserving* is her second book. Emily lives outside of Chicago with her husband and two children.

INDEX